THE ANTI-INFLAMMATORY DIET COOKBOOK 2024

Savor Balanced Recipes to Soothe Inflammation

Copyright©2024 Johnny M. Carr

All rights reserved. No part of this book may be reproduced

or used in any manner without the prior written permission

of the copyright owner, except for the use of brief quotations

in a book review.

Printed by Amazon in the USA.

Disclaimer : Although the author and publisher have made every effort to ensure that the information in this book was correct at press time, the author and publisher do not assume and hereby disclaim any liability to any party for any loss, damage, or disruption caused by errors or omissions, whether such errors or omissions result from negligence, accident, or any other cause. this book is not intended as a substitute for the medical advice of physicians.

TABLE OF CONTENTS

INTRODUCTION 5

DESSERTS & DRINKS RECIPES 14

Citrus, Turmeric, and Ginger Juice 14
Matcha Protein Shake 14
Protein Chia Pudding 15
5-Minute Pumpkin Spice Protein Shake 16
Green Protein Smoothie 16
One-Bowl Golden Glow Turmeric Flourless Muffins 17
Berry Protein Smoothie 18
Anti-Inflammatory Tropical Turmeric Popsicles 19
Matcha Collagen Cashew Butter 19
No-Bake Lemon Turmeric Energy Bites 20
Healthy Turmeric Chai Spiced Pumpkin Muffins 21
Fresh Turmeric Smoothie Bowl 22
Raspberry Chia Jam 22

POULTRY RECIPES 23

Skillet Chicken and Sweet Potatoes 23
Easy Italian Chicken Zucchini Skillet 24
Honey Orange Dijon Chicken Skewers 25
Spinach & Artichoke Casserole with Chicken and Cauliflower Rice 26
Salt & Vinegar Sheet-Pan Chicken & Brussels Sprouts 27
Slow-Cooker Chicken & White Bean Stew 28
Sheet-Pan Chicken Fajita Bowls 29
Adobo Chicken & Kale Enchiladas 30
Chicken Parmesan & Quinoa Stuffed Peppers 31
Instant Pot Thai Coconut Lime Chicken Soup with Noodles 32
Instant Pot Apricot Ginger Chicken Thighs with Bok Choy 34

BREAKFAST AND BRUNCH RECIPES 36

Artichoke Ricotta Flatbread. 36
Walnut Sage Pesto Pasta with Roasted Delicata Squash 37
Best Asian Garlic Paleo Whole30 Noodles 38
Spaghetti Squash with Asparagus, Ricotta, Lemon, and Thyme 39

Turmeric Milk 40

Protein Overnight Oats 41

Sweet Potato Hashbrown Egg Nests 42

DIY Greek Quinoa Bowl 43

Slow Cooker Enchilada Quinoa 44

Spinach & Artichoke Dip Pasta 45

20-Minute Balsamic Mushroom & Spinach Pasta 45

Creamy Spinach Pasta 46

Spinach, Lima Bean & Crispy Pancetta Pasta 47

Spicy Cauliflower Burrito Bowl 48

Strawberry-Chia Breakfast Pudding 49

Berry Baked Oatmeal 50

Savory Oatmeal With Spinach and Poached Eggs 50

Easy Sheet-Pan Dinner: Shawarma-Seasoned Cauliflower and Chickpea Pitas 51

Avocado Grain Bowl With Beet Ginger Dressing 52

Mole-Spiced Black Bean and Quinoa Bowl 53

This Anti-Inflammatory Berry Matcha Smoothie Is the Best Healthy Breakfast for Busy Mornings 54

SEAFOOD & FISH RECIPES 55

Salmon & Avocado Poke Bowl 55

Sheet-Pan Shrimp & Beets 55

Salmon Farro Salad with Corn and Bacon 56

Green Curry Salmon with Broccoli 58

Everything Crusted Tuna Meal Prep Bowls 59

Easy One Pan Mediterranean Cod 60

Mediterranean Sheet Pan Salmon with Zucchini Noodles 61

Halibut with Spiced Chickpeas and Carrots 62

Spicy Crunchy Salmon and Broccoli Sheet Pan Meal 63

Sun-Dried Tomato Butter Salmon and Broccolini Is Your New Go-To Easy Dinner 65

Salmon Tacos With Grapefruit Salsa 66

Smoky Sheet Pan Salmon and Potatoes 66

Soy-Glazed Salmon Sandwiches With Watercress 67

Sheet Pan Salmon With Potatoes and Broccolini 68

SIDE DISHES, SNACKS & VEGETARIAN RECIPES 69

Roasted Vegetable & Black Bean Tacos 69

Quinoa Chili with Sweet Potatoes 69

One-Pot Lemon-Broccoli Pasta with Parmesan 70

Buffalo Cauliflower Tacos 71

Roasted Root Veggies & Greens over Spiced Lentils. 72

Baked Eggs in Tomato Sauce with Kale 73

Black Bean-Quinoa Bowl 74

Chickpea & Quinoa Bowl with Roasted Red Pepper Sauce 74

Korean Seasoned Kale and Spinach 75

Beet Sumac Hummus 76

Thai Red Vegetable Curry 77

Creamy Pumpkin Cauliflower Curry with Chickpeas 78

Creamy Kale and Mushroom Stuffed Delicata Squash 79

This Tofu Fried Rice Recipe Is a Weeknight Dinner Must 80

Summer Squash Farro Bowl 81

Tofu and Mushroom Larb 82

Whole Roasted Cauliflower With Grapes and Feta 83

SOUPS, STEW & SALADS RECIPES 84

Slow Cooker Sweet Potato, Apple, & Turmeric Soup 84

Slow Cooker Butternut Squash, Kale & Quinoa Stew 85

Easy Slow Cooker Lentil Soup 86

Minestra Maritata (Italian Wedding Soup) 88

Hearty Chickpea & Spinach Stew 88

Kale & Avocado Salad with Blueberries & Edamame 90

One-Pot Lentil & Vegetable Soup with Parmesan 90

Egg Drop Soup with Instant Noodles, Spinach & Scallions 91

Slow-Cooker Mediterranean Diet Stew 92

Chicken & Kale Soup 93

Vegetable Soup 94

Thai Carrot Soup 95

Super Green Detoxifying Broccoli Soup 96

Greek Lentil Jar Salad 97

Escarole Citrus Salad with Meyer Lemon Vinaigrette 98

Farmers Market Lentil Salad 99

Mediterranean Farro Salad with Roasted Eggplant .100

Super Seed Salad Topper 101

Red Cabbage Vegetable Quinoa Stew 102

Spring Green Salad 103

Farro and Squash Salad 103

Coconut Ranch Kale Salad 104

Niçoise Salad 105

Burrata Salad 106

Greek Salmon Salad 107

INTRODUCTION

In the United States, chronic disease, like cardiovascular disease and diabetes, is the number one cause of death and disability. While chronic disease can take many forms, all share the common underlying cause: chronic, low-grade inflammation. Inflammation isn't always a bad thing, though. It's actually vital for survival. When you injure yourself or are trying to fight off a foreign invader (like a bacteria or virus), your immune system comes to the rescue with a variety of tools to clear the scene and ultimately restore homeostasis (balance). This type of acute inflammation allows you to survive and thrive despite the insult. However, when diet, lifestyle, and environmental factors trigger the inflammatory response unnecessarily, the resulting inflammatory cascade becomes chronic and, without intervention, can ultimately lead to the development of a disease. In order to quiet the response and prevent the damage caused by chronic inflammation, you must pinpoint and then target what's triggering the inflammatory response in the first place. In this article, we'll discuss the specifics of inflammation, what causes it, and tests that can help you identify it. We'll also dig into the anti-inflammatory diet and share the foods you'll want to avoid and the foods you'll want to bring in, as well as supplement options that help lower inflammation.

What is The Anti-Inflammatory Diet?

Food can affect the levels of inflammation in the body. Dietary patterns high in ultra-processed foods and low in nutrient-dense foods like fruits, vegetables, and whole grains tend to promote low-grade chronic inflammation that leads to disease development. On the other hand, an anti-inflammatory diet eliminates foods that can promote inflammation and instead focuses on foods that can prevent, reduce, or resolve it. The Mediterranean diet is currently the most well-studied anti-inflammatory diet. It has been shown to reduce levels of inflammatory biomarkers like interleukin-6 (IL-6). While it's not clear exactly why, the anti-inflammatory effect of this type of dietary pattern may be due to a variety of mechanisms like better blood sugar control, an improved gut microbiome profile, better immune system function, and lowered oxidative stress. Anti-inflammatory diets aren't one-size-fits-all and should be tailored to individual patient's needs. Essentially, any meal pattern that's built around fruits, vegetables, unsaturated fats, whole grains, legumes, tea, coffee, herbs, spices, and oily fish would be considered anti-inflammatory. This type of diet also limits or completely excludes foods that can contribute to inflammation like high-fat red and processed meats, ultra-processed foods, refined grains, sugary foods and beverages, and excessive amounts of alcohol. Food sensitivities are an additional consideration when planning an anti-inflammatory diet. Being sensitive to a certain food, whether it's considered to be anti-inflammatory or not, can contribute to low-grade inflammation. So, the anti-inflammatory diet will ideally be tailored around any food sensitivities.

What Are Some Medical Conditions The Anti-Inflammatory Diet is Prescribed for?

Since an anti-inflammatory diet can help to prevent chronic inflammation, it's a great idea for anyone to follow this way of eating. However, since chronic inflammation is a hallmark of most chronic diseases, people with conditions like obesity, metabolic syndrome, prediabetes and diabetes, autoimmune disease, cancer, arthritis, and cognitive decline are commonly prescribed an anti-inflammatory diet. Context is key when it comes to inflammation. There are two kinds: acute inflammation and chronic inflammation. Acute inflammation is a survival mechanism that the body uses to repair damaged tissue and to fight off infections. In an acute state (like a cut or sprained ankle), the immune system sends inflammatory cells (leukocytes) to the affected area with resulting symptoms like reddened skin, pain, swelling, and heat. Once the job is completed (this could take hours or days), the body then down-regulates these inflammatory mediators to restore balance. But, if the body isn't able to apply the brakes normally due to a continuous assault or a weakened immune system, these pro-inflammatory mediators continue to be released and can build up. This is where chronic inflammation comes into play and disease risk increases.

Symptoms of Inflammation

In chronic inflammation, some triggers, whether a microbe (like Helicobacter pylori), food, environment, or lifestyle, signals the immune system to send out pro-inflammatory mediators. This process can last much longer than the acute response, and over time, a buildup of reactive molecules can damage the tissues and organs of the body. People with chronic inflammation can experience symptoms that come and go like:

- Abdominal pain
- Chest pain
- Fatigue
- Fever
- Gastrointestinal distress
- Headaches
- Joint pain or stiffness
- Mouth sores
- Skin rash
- Weight gain

Functional Medicine Labs Commonly Used with The Anti-Inflammatory Diet

Testing for inflammation can be a challenge as common blood tests aren't always diagnostic. Along with traditional blood tests, integrative providers can use many tests to look for the root causes of inflammation, like poor gut function, food sensitivities, bacterial overgrowth, and glucose dysregulation. Here are some functional medicine labs that may help identify and treat inflammation.

Comprehensive Stool Test

The GI-Map stool test by Doctor's Data is a valuable test that analyzes stool samples for various markers of gastrointestinal health, including microbial imbalance, digestive enzyme levels, and inflammation. By identifying potential imbalances and digestive issues, this test can help to uncover the root causes of inflammation and guide targeted treatments to improve gut health and inflammation levels.

Food Sensitivity Testing

The Array-10 Multiple Food Immune Reactivity Screen by Cyrex Laboratories is a food sensitivity test that measures the body's immune response to various foods. This test analyzes blood samples for IgG and IgA antibodies against common food proteins. Food sensitivities may be one driver of inflammation, so identifying them and personalizing an anti-inflammatory diet may be one way to target inflammation better.

SIBO Testing

The SIBO Breath Test by Genova Diagnostics is a non-invasive test that measures hydrogen and methane gases in the breath to assess the presence of small intestinal bacterial overgrowth (SIBO). SIBO can lead to increased intestinal permeability, which can be a root cause of chronic, low-grade inflammation. Targeting SIBO with antibiotics, probiotics, and dietary changes may help to restore gut balance and reduce inflammation.

Diabetes Panel

Since hyperglycemia is a root cause of inflammation, it's essential to know if you have diabetes or prediabetes. The Diabetes Panel from Vibrant America measures biomarkers associated with the diagnosis of diabetes, like fasting insulin, fasting glucose, and hemoglobin A1c. With these tests, practitioners can make personalized nutrition and lifestyle recommendations to help patients normalize blood sugar and lower inflammation.

Additional Labs to Check

Traditional testing for inflammation can include four common blood tests.

Erythrocyte Sedimentation Rate (sed rate or ESR)

ESR measures how fast red blood cells settle. During inflammation, red blood cells fall faster. A typical normal value is less than 20mm/hr.

C-Reactive Protein (CRP)

CRP is made in the liver, this level tends to rise when inflammation is present. A typical normal value is less than 3mg/L.

Ferritin

Ferritin is a blood protein that reflects the iron stores in the body. When inflammation is present, ferritin levels rise. A typical normal value is 20 to 200mcg/L.

Fibrinogen

Fibrinogen is a protein that rises when inflammation is present. A typical normal value is 200 to 400 mg/dL. * None of these are necessarily diagnostic on their own and no test for inflammation is perfect. Lab values and test results should only be one component of an overall, comprehensive evaluation.

Foods to Eat on the Anti-Inflammatory Diet

Whole foods are the foundation of an anti-inflammatory diet. Let's take a look at specific foods and why they're included.

Fruits and Vegetables

Fruits and vegetables provide important phytonutrients, antioxidants, and fiber to help keep the gut microbiome balanced and reduce the inflammatory response. One study found close adherence to the Mediterranean diet improved the gut microbiome, which may explain some of its anti-inflammatory effects. In order to get the most nutrients, it's best to consume a wide variety of both fruits and vegetables.

Whole Grains

Whole grains contain phytonutrients, vitamins, minerals, and fiber and have been found to positively impact the gut microbiome, possibly leading to an anti-inflammatory benefit. Whole grains include barley, brown rice, bulgur, farro, millet, quinoa, oatmeal, popcorn, and whole wheat flour.

Fish

Foods that contain long-chain omega-3 fatty acids are an excellent option for lowering inflammation. The omega-3 fats found in fatty fish include eicosapentaenoic acid (EPA) and docosahexaenoic acid (DHA). Include two to three servings of fatty fish like salmon, mackerel, herring, trout, sardines, and tuna each week.

Healthy Fats

Healthy fats may help to lower inflammation in the body. For example, olive oil (a monounsaturated fat) contains antioxidants and polyphenols that are known to reduce proinflammatory mediators. Healthy fats to choose include olives and olive oil, avocados and avocado oil, nuts, and seeds.

Beans and Legumes

Beans and legumes contain a variety of polyphenols and fiber to help reduce inflammation. Include chickpeas, lentils, and a variety of beans into your diet to benefit from their heart-healthy properties.

Tea and Coffee

Green, white, black and oolong teas contain anti-inflammatory compounds like epigallocatechin gallate (EGCG), theasinensin A, and theaflavin, which have all been shown to reduce inflammatory mediators and inflammatory pathways in cancer patients. Coffee contains a variety of bioactive compounds thought to provide anti-oxidant and anti-inflammatory benefits, which is protective against a number of chronic diseases.

Herbs and Spices

Various herbs and spices have been found to reduce pro-inflammatory mediators to provide an anti-inflammatory effect. Add garlic, ginger, turmeric, cinnamon, and cayenne to your favorite dishes next time you cook.

Foods to Avoid on The Anti-Inflammatory Diet

While consuming anti-inflammatory foods is key to lowering inflammation, those benefits will be negated if inflammatory foods are routinely consumed. Here are the foods to avoid and why they should be avoided on an anti-inflammatory diet.

Ultra-Processed Foods, Sweets, and Sugary Beverages

High intakes of ultra-processed foods are associated with low-grade inflammation. This could be because of a condition known as gut dysbiosis or disruption of the gut microbiome, which promotes increased intestinal permeability, immune system dysregulation, and inflammation. Not only are ultra-processed foods high in calories, sodium, added sugars, potentially harmful additives, and potentially inflammatory fats, they're also low in vitamins, minerals, phytonutrients, and fiber. The most common ultra-processed foods include soft drinks and other sugar-sweetened beverages, processed bread, refined breakfast cereals, sugar-sweetened baked goods (cakes, pies, cookies, and brownies), pre-packaged sauces, frozen meals, and processed meats (hot dogs, salami, bacon, sausage, and pepperoni). Additional ultra-processed foods to avoid include processed foods made with high-fructose corn syrup or hydrogenated oils.

Inflammatory Fats

Trans fats, or partially hydrogenated oils, promote inflammation and occur naturally in small amounts in some foods like dairy and meat. Still, artificial trans fats (which have been banned in many countries) can be found in margarine, deep-fried foods, microwave popcorn, baked goods, pie crust, frozen pizza, cookies, and crackers. High intakes of saturated fats from full-fat dairy products, partially hydrogenated oils, and fatty cuts of red meat and poultry may also contribute to low-grade, chronic inflammation.

Refined Grains

Foods high in refined carbohydrates, like white flour, white rice, and white bread, are quickly broken down into simple sugars, which are more rapidly absorbed. This process may lead to hyperglycemia (high blood sugar), which is known to increase inflammation.

Alcohol

Consuming alcohol, especially in excess, can drive gut-derived inflammation by increasing intestinal permeability, altering immune system function, and changing the composition of gut microbes.

Supplements and Herbs that Lower Inflammation

Food is powerful, but there are several supplements and spices that integrative providers can use in combination with the anti-inflammatory diet to prevent or lower inflammation.

Ginger

Ginger has multiple bioactive compounds, such as gingerols, shogaols, paradols, and zingerone, which are responsible for its medicinal and anti-inflammatory effects. Ginger can modulate the immune system response and limit inflammatory pathways and has been shown to have anti-inflammatory effects similar to non-steroidal anti-inflammatory drugs.

Turmeric

Curcumin, the active compond found in turmeric and has been shown to down-regulate many pro-inflammatory mediators and cytokines with resulting benefits for a variety of chronic inflammatory diseases. Bioavailability can be improved when curcumin is combined with piperine (black pepper).

Probiotics

Probiotics provide their anti-inflammatory benefits in a number of ways. They produce short-chain fatty acids, which among other benefits can reduce inflammation in the colon. Probiotics also upregulate polypeptides that lower inflammation, and play a role in tryptophan metabolism, which ultimately increases the production of anti-inflammatory cytokines.

Summary

Acute inflammation is a protective mechanism that helps us recover from an injury or illness. However, we can develop chronic low-grade inflammation when the acute inflammatory response goes on longer than it should either from poor immune system function or a continuous trigger. This type of persistent inflammation is a root cause of many chronic diseases like diabetes, autoimmunity, cardiovascular disease, and cancer. If you already have, or are hoping to prevent a chronic disease, food is one powerful way to prevent, reduce, or resolve inflammation in the body. An anti-inflammatory diet, like the Mediterranean diet, is built around a wide variety of fruits and vegetables, whole grains, fish, healthy fats, beans, legumes, herbs, spices, tea, and coffee. All of these contain various nutrients, phytonutrients, and fiber to help reverse the inflammatory process. The anti-inflammatory diet also strictly limits or even excludes inflammatory foods like ultra-processed foods, inflammatory fats, refined grains, and alcohol, and also takes food sensitivities into consideration. In addition to using food as inflammation-fighting medicine, integrative providers may use targeted supplements like probiotics, ginger, and turmeric.

DESSERTS & DRINKS RECIPES

Citrus, Turmeric, and Ginger Juice

Servings: 1

Ingredients:

- 2 Fuji apples, cored and sliced
- 1 orange, peeled and sectioned
- ½ lemon, peeled
- 1 (1 inch) piece fresh ginger
- ½ teaspoon ground turmeric

Directions:

1. Process apples, orange, lemon, and ginger through a juicer; stir in turmeric until evenly incorporated.

Nutrition Facts:

Calories 163 Total Fat 1g Saturated Fat 0g Sodium 6mg Total Carbohydrate 46g Dietary Fiber 10g Total Sugars 29g Protein 2g Vitamin C 56mg Calcium 54mg Iron 1mg Potassium 428mg

Matcha Protein Shake

Servings: 1

Ingredients:

- 1 frozen banana broken into chunks
- 2 teaspoons matcha powder
- 1 cup packed baby spinach
- 1 tablespoon ground flax seed
- 1 cup unsweetened milk of choice
- 1 serving vanilla protein powder plant-based protein powder for vegan
- optional: ice

Directions:

2. Add all the ingredients to a high speed blender. Blend on high until smooth.

Notes

Add 2 teaspoons pure maple syrup or 1-2 pitted Medjool dates if you prefer a sweeter protein shake.

If using fresh banana instead of frozen, add ice for better texture.

For a thinner consistency, add more milk.

For nut-free be sure to use a nut-free milk like oat milk, coconut milk or hemp milk.

For vegan, be sure to use a plant-based protein powder. For paleo, be sure to use a paleo-friendly protein powder. Nutrition information calculated using almond milk and protein powder. Nutrition information will depend on the type of protein powder you use.

Nutrition Facts:

Calories: 308kcal | Carbohydrates: 4g | Protein: 25g | Fat: 3g | Saturated Fat: 0.3g | Polyunsaturated Fat: 2g | Monounsaturated Fat: 1g | Cholesterol: 2mg | Sodium: 352mg | Potassium: 231mg | Fiber: 3g | Sugar: 1g | Vitamin A: 3216IU | Vitamin C: 9mg | Calcium: 351mg | Iron: 3mg

Protein Chia Pudding

Cooking Time: 3 Hours

Servings: 1

Ingredients:

- 2 tablespoons chia seeds
- ½ cup plus 2 tablespoons unsweetened almond milk or milk of choice
- 1 scoop protein powder of choice
- 2 teaspoons liquid sweetener of choice such as maple syrup or honey (optional)
- Suggested Toppings
- 1 tablespoon nut or seed butter, fresh strawberries, fresh blueberries

Directions:

3. To an 8-ounce wide mason jar, or other jar with tightly fitting lid, add 2 tablespoons chia seeds and one scoop of protein powder, stirring with a fork to combine.
4. Add the milk and sweetener, if using. Secure the lid, then shake vigorously until all the ingredients have combined and protein powder dissolves.
5. Allow to sit for 5 minutes, then shake vigorously again.
6. Allow to sit an additional 5 minutes, shake vigorously, then refrigerate for at least 3 hours or up to 5 days, covered.
7. Serve chilled or at room temperature, with nut butter and fresh berries if desired.

Notes

Nutrition facts calculated without optional sweetener or toppings, the protein content will depend on the protein powder you use.

Most commercial protein powders contain sweetener, but if you like a sweeter pudding, feel free to add the optional sweetener.

This recipe can easily be multiplied based on the number of Servings: you need.

Nutrition Facts:

Calories: 254kcal | Carbohydrates: 14g | Protein: 30g | Fat: 11g | Saturated Fat: 1g | Polyunsaturated Fat: 6g | Monounsaturated Fat: 1g | Trans Fat: 1g | Cholesterol: 50mg | Sodium: 211mg | Potassium: 188mg | Fiber: 9g | Sugar: 2g | Vitamin A: 93IU | Vitamin C: 1mg | Calcium: 399mg | Iron: 4mg

5-Minute Pumpkin Spice Protein Shake

Cooking Time: 5 Minutes

Servings: 2

Ingredients:

- 1 cup frozen riced cauliflower
- ¾ cup pumpkin puree
- 1/3 cup unsweetened greek yogurt
- 1 tablespoon almond butter
- 1 teaspoon pumpkin pie spice
- 1 serving vanilla protein powder (or pumpkin spice protein powder)
- 3/4 cup unsweetened almond milk (or milk of choice)
- Optional Toppings
- whipped cream or coconut cream
- pumpkin pie spice

Directions:

1. Add all the ingredients to a high speed blender. Blend until smooth.

Notes

For nut-free, use sunflower seed butter.

For vegan, use a plant-based yogurt and protein powder.

Nutrition Facts:

Serving: 1(of 2) | Calories: 195kcal | Carbohydrates: 12g | Protein: 22g | Fat: 7g | Saturated Fat: 1g | Polyunsaturated Fat: 2g | Monounsaturated Fat: 3g | Cholesterol: 32mg | Sodium: 102mg | Potassium: 603mg | Fiber: 6g | Sugar: 5g | Vitamin A: 14303IU | Vitamin C: 43mg | Calcium: 302mg | Iron: 2mg

Green Protein Smoothie

Servings: 2

Ingredients:

- 1 frozen banana
- 2 cups baby spinach
- 1 tablespoon chia seeds
- 1 cup unsweetened milk of choice such as almond or cashew milk
- 1 scoop vanilla protein powder
- 1 tablespoon peanut butter

Directions:

2. Add all the ingredients to a high speed blender. Blend on high until smooth.

Nutrition Facts:

Serving: 1 (of 2) | Calories: 159kcal | Carbohydrates: 9g | Protein: 14g | Fat: 9g | Saturated Fat: 1g | Polyunsaturated Fat: 3g | Monounsaturated Fat: 3g | Trans Fat: 0.01g | Cholesterol: 31mg | Sodium: 160mg | Potassium: 300mg | Fiber: 4g | Sugar: 2g | Vitamin A: 2817IU | Vitamin C: 9mg | Calcium: 298mg | Iron: 1mg

One-Bowl Golden Glow Turmeric Flourless Muffins

Servings: 12

Ingredients:

- 1/3 cup melted coconut oil plus more for greasing the pan
- 2 large eggs
- 2/3 cup unsweetened applesauce
- 1/3 cup pure maple syrup
- 1 teaspoon vanilla extract
- 2 1/3 cups almond or oat flour*
- ½ teaspoon baking soda
- ½ teaspoon baking powder
- ¼ teaspoon kosher salt
- 2 teaspoons ground turmeric
- ½ teaspoon cinnamon
- ½ teaspoon ground ginger
- ⅛ teaspoon freshly ground pepper**
- 1/3 cup dairy-free chocolate chips plus more for sprinkling

Directions:

3. Heat the oven to 350F.
4. In a large bowl, whisk together the coconut oil, eggs, applesauce, maple syrup, and vanilla extract.
5. Add the flour, baking soda, baking powder, salt, turmeric, cinnamon, ginger, and pepper. Stir until well incorporated.
6. Add the chocolate chips, stirring to combine.
7. Fill each section of a greased, 12-section muffin tin with roughly ¼ cup batter. Sprinkle the tops with chocolate chips, then bake for 15-20 minutes, or until the edges begin to pull away from the sides and a toothpick comes out clean.
8. Allow to cool in the pan for 5 minutes, then cool the rest on a cooling rack.

Notes

*Make your own oat flour for this recipe by placing 2 1/3 cups whole rolled oats in a blender and blending until a coarse flour forms.

The pepper helps to activate the turmeric.

You can purchase pre-made oat flour at many grocery stores and natural food markets or online. If you are gluten-free be sure to buy oats that are specifically labeled gluten-free.

These muffins can also be made into a quick bread. Simply add to a greased loaf pan and cook for 45-50 minutes, or until a toothpick comes out clean.

Invite the little ones into the kitchen to help with the prep. They can stir the batter, and help spoon it into the muffin tins! These muffins freeze well. Just cool completely, then store in a tightly sealing zip-top bag for up to 3 months.

Berry Protein Smoothie

Servings: 2

Ingredients:

- 1 cup frozen mixed berries (or any combination of strawberries, raspberries, blueberries and blackberries)
- 1 tbsp chia seeds
- 1 tbsp unsweetened almond butter (or nut butter of choice or use seed butter for nut-free)
- 2 tbsp vanilla protein powder
- 1 tbsp fresh lemon juice
- 1 cup unsweetened almond milk (or milk of choice)

Directions:

1. Add all the ingredients to a high speed blender. Blend on high until well smooth. Serve immediately.

Notes

This recipe makes about 2 cups, or two Servings: if using a serving size of 1 cup.

To make a berry protein smoothie bowl make the smoothie thicker by using ¾ cup milk.

For a thinner consistency, add more milk.

If using fresh berries, add extra ice for better texture.

Nutrition information calculated with almond milk, protein information will depend on the type of protein powder you use.

Nutrition Facts:

Calories: 191kcal | Carbohydrates: 17g | Protein: 13g | Fat: 9g | Saturated Fat: 1g | Polyunsaturated Fat: 3g | Monounsaturated Fat: 4g | Trans Fat: 1g | Cholesterol: 29mg | Sodium: 201mg | Potassium: 191mg | Fiber: 5g | Sugar: 8g | Vitamin A: 39IU | Vitamin C: 5mg | Calcium: 294mg | Iron: 1mg

Anti-Inflammatory Tropical Turmeric Popsicles

Servings: 6

Ingredients:

- 3 cups of chopped pineapple about 3/4 of a fresh pineapple
- 2 tsp turmeric
- 1/2 tsp black pepper
- 2 tbsp coconut oil
- 2 kiwi sliced

Directions:

2. In a blender combine pineapple, turmeric, black pepper, and coconut oil. I blended until smooth, but if you like a popsicle with more texture keep some pineapple chunks intact.
3. Pour into a popsicle mold, slide sliced kiwi into molds.
4. Freeze for 24 hours.
5. Tada! You just made popsicles!

Nutrition Facts:

Calories: 101kcal | Carbohydrates: 15g | Fat: 4g | Saturated Fat: 3g | Sodium: 2mg | Potassium: 203mg | Fiber: 2g | Sugar: 10g | Vitamin A: 75IU | Vitamin C: 67.7mg | Calcium: 21mg | Iron: 0.6mg

Matcha Collagen Cashew Butter

Cooking Time: 5 Mins.

Servings: 16

Ingredients:

- 2 cups raw cashews
- 1 scoop matcha collagen powder or 1 tsp matcha green tea powder

Directions:

1. Add cashews to the bowl of a food processor and blend for 3-5 minutes, stopping every minute or so to scrape down the sides. Be patient at first it will look like cashew dust, it takes time for the cashews to release their natural oils. After it becomes creamy add one scoop of matcha collagen powder or 1 tsp of matcha powder and 1 scoop of collagen powder. Process until well incorporated.
2. Will keep for 1 month in the fridge.

Notes

You can use any nut you like, but I think cashews work the best in this recipe

You can sub 1 tsp matcha powder and your favorite protein powder

Nutrition Facts:

Serving: 1serving | Calories: 92kcal | Carbohydrates: 5g | Protein: 3g | Fat: 7g | Saturated Fat: 1g | Sodium: 5mg

| Potassium: 106mg | Sugar: 1g | Vitamin C: 0.1mg | Calcium: 6mg | Iron: 1.1mg

No-Bake Lemon Turmeric Energy Bites

Servings: 30

Ingredients:

- 2 cups raw nuts cashews, walnuts, pecans
- 1 cup dessicated coconut
- 1/4 cup coconut butter
- 3/4 tsp turmeric
- 1/4 cup lemon juice
- 1 tbsp lemon zest
- 2 scoops collagen peptides
- pinch sea salt and black pepper
- (optional) toppings
- shredded coconut and lemon zest (about 1 tsp lemon zest and 1/4 cup shredded coconut)

Directions:

1. In the bowl of a food processor pulse nuts until they resemble a dry flour. Add all remaining ingredients and pulse until resembling a dough. (note: if your coconut butter is super firm you may need to heat it to add to the mixture)
2. Roll dough into small balls between the palms of your hand, roll in shredded coconut and lemon zest.
3. As you roll dough it will produce more oil, I gently rolled the balls over a paper towel to remove some of the oil and then rolled in coconut and lemon.
4. Store in airtight container in the fridge for 3-4 weeks, but they will never last that long ;-)

Notes

Make sure to use unsweetened shredded coconut

If you don't have coconut butter, coconut oil will also work but will produce a different texture

I used collagen peptides as my protein powder but you could easily sub for a vegan protein powder or leave it out entirely

Nutrition information is based on 1 energy bite

Nutrition Facts:

Calories: 78kcal | Carbohydrates: 3g | Protein: 2g | Fat: 6g | Saturated Fat: 2g | Sodium: 9mg | Potassium: 77mg | Fiber: 1g | Vitamin C: 1.2mg | Calcium: 5mg | Iron: 0.9mg

Healthy Turmeric Chai Spiced Pumpkin Muffins

Cooking Time: 18 Mins.

Servings: 12

Ingredients:

- 1 cup rolled oats
- 1 cup brown rice flour
- 1 1/2 tsp baking soda
- 3/4 tsp salt
- 1 1/4 tbsp turmeric chai spice
- 1 cup pumpkin puree
- 2 large eggs
- 1/3 cup oat milk or any plant or cow milk
- 1/2 cup maple syrup
- 2 tbsp coconut oil
- 1/2 tsp vanilla extract
- 1/2 tsp almond extract
- Turmeric Chai Spice
- 1 tsp ground ginger
- 1 tsp ground cardamom
- 1/2 tsp turmeric
- 1/4 tsp allspice
- 1/4 tsp nutmeg
- 1/4 tsp clove
- 1/8 tsp ground black pepper

Directions:

1. Preheat oven to 350° and prepare a 12 cup muffin tin with parchment liners or lightly spray with coconut oil spray. Set aside.
2. To make turmeric spice combine all spices and stir together (you can make a double or triple batch and use for other recipes). Set aside.
3. Prepare oat flour by placing rolled oats in a food processor or high-speed blender and processing until they are the consistency of silky flour.
4. In a medium bowl combine oat flour, brown rice flour, baking soda, salt, and turmeric chai spice. Whisk to combine.
5. In a larger bowl combine pumpkin puree, eggs, milk, maple syrup, melted coconut oil, vanilla and almond extract. Whisk well to combine.
6. Pour dry ingredients into wet and stir together until just combined (do not overmix).
7. Fill your muffin cups with the batter. Bake for 18-20 minutes or until a toothpick inserted in the center comes out clean. Allow to cool on wire rack for 10 minutes
8. Serve warm or room temperature. Store in a sealed container for 5 days or freeze for 3+ months.

Notes

You can replace the turmeric chai spice with 1 tbsp pumpkin pie spice plus 1/2 tsp of turmeric

You can also make the recipe using all oats and remove the brown rice flour, I liked the texture better with the mixed flours.

Oat milk can be replaced with any milk

Nutrition Facts:

Serving: 1muffin | Calories: 154kcal | Carbohydrates: 26g | Protein: 3g | Fat: 4g | Saturated Fat: 2g | Cholesterol: 31mg | Sodium: 321mg | Potassium: 149mg | Fiber: 2g | Sugar: 9g | Vitamin A: 3235IU | Vitamin C: 0.8mg | Calcium: 39mg | Iron: 1.1mg

Fresh Turmeric Smoothie Bowl

Servings: 12

Ingredients:

- 1 cup frozen cauliflower
- 1 cup frozen mango
- 1 orange
- 1/2 lemon
- 1 inch piece of fresh turmeric
- 1 tsp camu camu powder
- 1 tbsp coconut butter or coconut oil will do
- pinch of black pepper
- 1/2 cup water or more depending on consistency you'd like
- 1 scoop collagen peptides optional, or you can use any protein powder you like
- Toppings:
- coconut
- golden berries
- mango
- bee pollen

Directions:

1. Blend all ingredients until thick and smooth. Top with desired (optional) toppings

Notes

You may replace the collagen peptides with your protein powder of choice

Nutrition Facts:

Calories: 24kcal | Carbohydrates: 4g | Sodium: 3mg | Potassium: 75mg | Sugar: 3g | Vitamin A: 175IU | Vitamin C: 17.5mg | Calcium: 9mg | Iron: 0.1mg

Raspberry Chia Jam

Servings: 4

Ingredients:

- 1/3 cup orange juice or white grape juice
- 3 tablespoons chia seeds
- 2 ½ cups raspberries
- 3 to 4 tablespoons agave nectar

Directions:

2. Combine the juice and chia seeds in a blender. Let mixture soak 10 minutes. Add the raspberries and agave nectar. Blend until mostly smooth. To store, transfer jam to an airtight container and refrigerate for up to a week and a half.

POULTRY RECIPES

Skillet Chicken and Sweet Potatoes

Cooking Time: 25 Minutes

Servings: 4

Ingredients:

- 1 pound chicken thighs about 4 chicken thighs, or boneless, skinless chicken breast cut into large pieces
- 1 teaspoon salt divided
- 1 ½ pounds sweet potatoes cut into ½ inch pieces
- 2 tablespoons avocado oil divided (or other neutral flavored oil)
- 2 tablespoons butter or plant-based butter for dairy-free
- 2 tablespoons honey
- 1 teaspoon chipotle from a can of chipotle peppers in adobo, minced
- 1 garlic clove minced or finely grated

Directions:

3. Preheat the oven to 350F.
4. Sprinkle the chicken on both sides with ½ teaspoon salt.
5. Heat 1 tablespoon of avocado oil in a large, 12-inch skillet over medium-high heat.
6. Add the chicken and allow it to brown 3-4 minutes one one side. Flip and cook for an additional 3-4 minutes, or until browned. Remove to a plate and set aside.
7. Turn the heat down to medium, add the remaining 1 tablespoon avocado oil along with the sweet potatoes. Sprinkle with ½ teaspoon salt, and cook for 5 minutes, stirring frequently.
8. Meanwhile, melt the butter, honey, chipotle, and garlic together, either in the microwave or on the stovetop.
9. When the potatoes are slightly browned, add back the chicken along with any accumulated juices. Pour over the honey and butter mixture, stirring to combine.
10. Place in the oven and bake for 10-15 minutes, or until the chicken is cooked through and no longer pink in the middle.

Notes

This recipe serves 4 people with ¼ pounds of chicken per person. If you prefer more meat per serving, double the recipe or double the amount of chicken.

While the chipotle adds a nice little kick to this recipe, if you don't have it, don't want to use it, or are sensitive to heat, feel free to omit it.

Alternatively, if you like things spicy, double the chipotle. Nutrition information calculated using chicken thighs, avocado oil, and butter.

Nutrition Facts:

Calories: 544kcal | Carbohydrates: 44g | Protein: 21g | Fat: 32g | Saturated Fat: 10g | Polyunsaturated Fat: 5g | Monounsaturated Fat: 14g | Trans Fat: 1g | Cholesterol: 126mg | Sodium: 765mg | Potassium: 816mg | Fiber: 5g | Sugar: 16g | Vitamin A: 24395IU | Vitamin C: 4mg | Calcium: 64mg | Iron: 2mg

Easy Italian Chicken Zucchini Skillet

Cooking Time: 19 Minutes

Servings: 4

Ingredients:

- 2 tbsp olive oil divided
- 1 lb boneless, skinless chicken breasts or thighs cut into 1 inch pieces
- 1 tsp no-salt added Italian seasoning
- 1 tsp kosher salt divided
- 4 cups 1-inch diced zucchini (from about 4 medium zucchini)
- 2 garlic cloves finely minced or grated
- 1 15-oz can diced tomatoes
- 1 tbsp tomato paste
- 1/2 cup chicken stock
- 2 tbsp butter*
- 1/4 cup lightly packed fresh basil thinly sliced
- red pepper flakes to taste

Directions:

1. In a large 12-inch skillet, heat 1 tablespoon olive oil over medium high heat. Add the chicken in one layer, taking care not to overlap the pieces. Sprinkle with the Italian seasoning and ½ teaspoon salt.

2. Cook the chicken undisturbed, until golden brown on one side, about 5 minutes. Flip, and cook an additional 3 minutes until browned on both sides and just cooked through. Remove from the pan and set aside.

3. In the same pan, heat the remaining 1 tablespoon olive oil over medium heat. Add the zucchini, sprinkle with ½ teaspoon salt, and cook until just tender, stirring occasionally, about 5 minutes.

4. Add the garlic, and cook until fragrant, about 1 minutes, stirring occasionally.

5. Add chicken stock, stirring to deglaze, then add tomato paste and diced tomatoes, stirring until well

combined.

6. Add the cooked chicken back to the pan, turn the heat to medium low, and simmer uncovered for 5 minutes, until the sauce is slightly reduced.
7. Turn off the heat, add the butter, and stir to combine. Taste the sauce and add additional salt if desired. Serve sprinkled with basil and red pepper flakes to taste.

Notes

*Use dairy-free butter to keep this recipe dairy-free, or omit for Whole30.

This recipe works with either chicken breasts or thighs - if you prefer juicer chicken, use chicken thighs.

Nutrition Facts:

Calories: 298kcal | Carbohydrates: 11g | Protein: 28g | Fat: 17g | Saturated Fat: 5g | Polyunsaturated Fat: 2g | Monounsaturated Fat: 8g | Trans Fat: 1g | Cholesterol: 89mg | Sodium: 995mg | Potassium: 1027mg | Fiber: 3g | Sugar: 7g | Vitamin A: 727IU | Vitamin C: 35mg | Calcium: 75mg | Iron: 2mg

Honey Orange Dijon Chicken Skewers

Cooking Time: 8 Minutes

Servings: 3 -6

Ingredients:

- For the Honey Orange Dijon Sauce
- 3 tbsp Dijon mustard
- 2 tbsp honey (omit for Whole30)
- 1/4 cup fresh squeezed orange juice (from about 1 medium orange)
- 1/4 cup olive oil
- 1/2 tsp kosher salt
- 1/4 tsp freshly ground pepper
- 1 tbsp minced fresh sage
- For the Honey Orange Dijon Chicken Skewers
- 6 10-inch bamboo skewers presoaked
- 2 lbs boneless, skinless chicken thighs excess fat trimmed, and cut into 1-inch chunks

Directions:

1. In a medium bowl or mason jar, combine the mustard, honey, orange juice, olive oil, salt, pepper and sage, whisking or shaking until well combined.
2. Place the cubed chicken in a bowl. Add half the sauce and marinade for at least an hour, or all day

in the refrigerator, covered.

3. Remove the chicken from the marinade, shaking off any excess. Thread onto bamboo skewers. Discard extra marinade.
4. Preheat the grill to medium-high heat (about 400F). When the grill is hot, place the skewers on the grill and cook for 7-8 minutes, flipping halfway, until the chicken is cooked through and grill marks have formed.
5. Serve with remaining sauce, atop rice, and slaw if you prefer.

Notes

Rosemary would work in place of sage

Chicken breasts work in place of thighs, though will be drier

Spinach & Artichoke Casserole with Chicken and Cauliflower Rice

Servings: 4

Ingredients:

- 1 tablespoon extra-virgin olive oil
- 1 pound boneless, skinless chicken breasts, cut into bite-size pieces
- ¼ teaspoon salt
- ¼ teaspoon ground pepper
- 2 cloves garlic, minced
- 1 (14 ounce) can artichoke hearts, rinsed and chopped
- 4 cups fresh or frozen cauliflower rice (see Tip)
- 3 cups coarsely chopped fresh spinach
- 4 ounces reduced-fat cream cheese
- 1 cup shredded dill Havarti cheese, divided
- 1 tablespoon chopped fresh dill

Directions:

1. Preheat oven to 375°F. Lightly coat a 9-by-13-inch baking dish with cooking spray.
2. Heat oil in a large pot over medium heat. Add chicken, sprinkle with salt and pepper and cook, stirring, until opaque on all sides, about 8 minutes. Add garlic and cook, stirring, for 1 minute. Remove from heat.
3. Pat artichokes dry. Add to the pot along with cauliflower rice, spinach, cream cheese and ½ cup dill Havarti. Mix until the cream cheese is melted.
4. Transfer the mixture to the prepared baking dish and sprinkle with the remaining ½ cup dill Havarti. Bake until the cheese is melted, about 20 minutes. Remove from oven and let stand for 5 minutes. Sprinkle with dill before serving.

Tip

Look for prepared cauliflower rice with other prepared vegetables in the supermarket produce or freezer section. To make your own, place cauliflower florets in a food processor and pulse until broken down into rice-size granules. One 2-pound head of cauliflower yields about 4 cups of cauliflower rice. If using frozen cauliflower rice, be sure to thaw and pat dry to remove excess moisture.

Recipe Updates

Removed the chicken broth (to reduce the amount of liquid).

Swapped the mozzarella cheese for dill Havarti (to boost flavor).

Added fresh dill (to boost flavor).

Swapped the Greek yogurt for reduced-fat cream cheese (for a creamier texture).

Nutrition Facts:

Calories 428 Total Carbohydrate 14g Dietary Fiber 5g Total Sugars 3g Protein 39g Total Fat 22g Saturated Fat 11g Cholesterol 136mg Vitamin A 3678iu Sodium 776mg Potassium 387mg

Salt & Vinegar Sheet-Pan Chicken & Brussels Sprouts

Servings: 4

Ingredients:

- 1 ½ pounds bone-in, skin-on chicken breasts
- 3 tablespoons extra-virgin olive oil, divided
- 1 teaspoon kosher salt, divided
- ½ teaspoon ground pepper, divided
- 1 ½ pounds Brussels sprouts, trimmed and halved or quartered if large
- 2 medium red onions, cut into 1/2-inch wedges
- 6 tablespoons malt vinegar or sherry vinegar
- ½ teaspoon dried dill
- ½ teaspoon garlic powder
- ½ teaspoon onion powder
- ¼ teaspoon sugar

Directions:

1. Preheat oven to 450 degrees F.
2. Cut chicken breasts into 4 equal portions. Brush with 1 tablespoon oil and sprinkle with 1/4 teaspoon each salt and pepper. Toss Brussels sprouts and onions in a large bowl with the remaining 2 tablespoons oil and 1/4 teaspoon each salt and pepper. Arrange the vegetables and the

chicken in a single layer on a rimmed baking sheet.

3. Roast until an instant-read thermometer inserted in the thickest part of a breast without touching bone registers 160 degrees F and the vegetables are tender, 20 to 25 minutes.
4. Meanwhile, mix vinegar, dill, garlic powder, onion powder, sugar and the remaining 1/2 teaspoon salt in a small microwave-safe bowl. Microwave on High until the salt and sugar dissolve, about 30 seconds.
5. Drizzle the vinegar mixture over the chicken and vegetables and roast for 5 minutes more. Transfer the chicken to a serving platter and stir the vegetables on the pan. Serve the vegetables with the chicken.

Nutrition Facts:

Calories 387 Total Carbohydrate 20g   Dietary Fiber 7g   Total Sugars 6g   Protein 36g   Total Fat 19g   Saturated Fat 4g   Cholesterol 83mg   Vitamin A 1257iu   Vitamin C 134mg   Folate 108mcg   Sodium 592mg   Calcium 96mg   Iron 3mg   Magnesium 69mg   Potassium 934mg

Slow-Cooker Chicken & White Bean Stew

Servings: 6

Ingredients:

- 1 pound dried cannellini beans, soaked overnight and drained (see Tip, above)
- 6 cups unsalted chicken broth
- 1 cup chopped yellow onion
- 1 cup sliced carrots
- 1 teaspoon finely chopped fresh rosemary
- 1 (4 ounce) Parmesan cheese rind plus 2/3 cup grated Parmesan, divided
- 2 bone-in chicken breasts (1 pound each)
- 4 cups chopped kale
- 1 tablespoon lemon juice
- ½ teaspoon kosher salt
- ½ teaspoon ground pepper
- 2 tablespoons extra-virgin olive oil
- ¼ cup flat-leaf parsley leaves

Directions:

1. Combine beans, broth, onion, carrots, rosemary and Parmesan rind in a 6-quart slow cooker. Top with chicken. Cover and cook on Low until the beans and vegetables are tender, 7 to 8 hours.

2. Transfer the chicken to a clean cutting board; let stand until cool enough to handle, about 10 minutes. Shred the chicken, discarding bones.
3. Return the chicken to the slow cooker and stir in kale. Cover and cook on High until the kale is tender, 20 to 30 minutes.
4. Stir in lemon juice, salt and pepper; discard the Parmesan rind. Serve the stew drizzled with oil and sprinkled with Parmesan and parsley.

Nutrition Facts:

Calories 493　Total Carbohydrate 54g　Dietary Fiber 27g　Total Sugars 5g　Protein 44g　Total Fat 11g　Saturated Fat 3g　Cholesterol 68mg　Vitamin A 4793iu　Vitamin C 20mg　Folate 32mcg　Sodium 518mg　Calcium 199mg　Iron 7mg　Magnesium 149mg　Potassium 1557mg

Sheet-Pan Chicken Fajita Bowls

Servings: 4

Ingredients:

- 2 teaspoons chili powder
- 2 teaspoons ground cumin
- ¾ teaspoon salt, divided
- ½ teaspoon garlic powder
- ½ teaspoon smoked paprika
- ¼ teaspoon ground pepper
- 2 tablespoons olive oil, divided
- 1 ¼ pounds chicken tenders
- 1 medium yellow onion, sliced
- 1 medium red bell pepper, sliced
- 1 medium green bell pepper, sliced
- 4 cups chopped stemmed kale
- 1 (15 ounce) can no-salt-added black beans, rinsed
- ¼ cup low-fat plain Greek yogurt
- 1 tablespoon lime juice
- 2 teaspoons water

Directions:

1. Place a large rimmed baking sheet in the oven; preheat to 425 degrees F.
2. Combine chili powder, cumin, 1/2 tsp. salt, garlic powder, paprika, and ground pepper in a large bowl. Transfer 1 tsp. of the spice mixture to a medium bowl and set aside. Whisk 1 Tbsp. oil into the remaining spice mixture in the large bowl. Add chicken, onion, and red and green bell peppers; toss to coat.
3. Remove the pan from the oven; coat with cooking spray. Spread the chicken mixture in an even layer on the pan. Roast for 15 minutes.
4. Meanwhile, combine kale and black beans with the

remaining 1/4 tsp. salt and 1 Tbsp. olive oil in a large bowl; toss to coat.

5. Remove the pan from the oven. Stir the chicken and vegetables. Spread kale and beans evenly over the top. Roast until the chicken is cooked through and the vegetables are tender, 5 to 7 minutes more.
6. Meanwhile, add yogurt, lime juice, and water to the reserved spice mixture; stir to combine.
7. Divide the chicken and vegetable mixture among 4 bowls. Drizzle with the yogurt dressing and serve.

Tips

Tip: For easier weeknight prep, slice vegetables the night before; cover and refrigerate.

To make ahead: Prepare spice mixture (Step 1) up to 2 days ahead; store in an airtight container.

Nutrition Facts:

Calories 343 Total Carbohydrate 24g Dietary Fiber 8g Total Sugars 4g Protein 43g Total Fat 10g Saturated Fat 1g Cholesterol 71mg Vitamin A 2775iu Vitamin C 73mg Folate 25mcg Sodium 605mg Calcium 187mg Iron 4mg Magnesium 63mg Potassium 580mg

Adobo Chicken & Kale Enchiladas

Servings: 5

Ingredients:

- 1 tablespoon extra-virgin olive oil
- 8 cups chopped kale
- ¼ cup water
- 2 cups shredded or diced cooked chicken
- 1 teaspoon ground cumin
- ¼ teaspoon salt
- ¼ teaspoon ground pepper
- 1 (10 ounce) can red enchilada sauce (1 1/4 cups)
- ¼ cup sour cream
- 2-3 tablespoons minced chipotles in adobo
- 12 corn tortillas
- ¾ cup diced white onion, divided
- 1 ½ cups shredded Mexican blend cheese, divided

Directions:

1. Preheat oven to 450 degrees F.
2. Heat oil in a large cast-iron skillet (12-inch) over medium-high heat. Add kale and water; cook, stirring, until bright green and wilted, about 2 minutes. Stir in chicken, cumin, salt and pepper; cook for 1 minute more. Transfer to a large bowl.
3. Combine enchilada sauce, sour cream and chipotles to taste in a small bowl. Spread 1/2 cup of the

mixture in the pan. Place 4 tortillas over the sauce, overlapping them to cover the bottom. Top with half the chicken mixture, 1/4 cup onion and 1/2 cup cheese. Layer on half the remaining sauce, 4 tortillas, the remaining chicken, 1/4 cup onion and 1/2 cup cheese. Top with the remaining tortillas, sauce and cheese.

4. Bake the enchiladas until bubbling, 12 to 15 minutes. Sprinkle with the remaining 1/4 cup onion before serving.

Nutrition Facts:

Calories 415 Total Carbohydrate 35g Dietary Fiber 6g Total Sugars 4g Protein 32g Total Fat 18g Saturated Fat 8g Cholesterol 71mg Vitamin A 3232iu Vitamin C 33mg Folate 51mcg Sodium 653mg Calcium 344mg Iron 2mg Magnesium 69mg Potassium 367mg

Chicken Parmesan & Quinoa Stuffed Peppers

Servings: 4

Ingredients:

- 1 tablespoon olive oil
- 1 medium onion, chopped (about 1 1/2 cups)
- 4 cloves garlic, minced
- 1 cup quinoa, rinsed
- 1 ¼ cups water
- 3 cups shredded cooked chicken breast
- 1 ½ cups lower-sodium marinara sauce
- 1/3 cup grated Parmesan cheese
- ¾ cup sliced fresh basil, divided
- 4 large red bell peppers (about 8 ounces each)
- 2 ounces low-moisture, part-skim mozzarella cheese, shredded (about 1/2 cup)

Directions:

1. Preheat oven to 350 degrees F. Heat oil in a medium saucepan over medium-high heat. Add onion and garlic; cook, stirring occasionally, until the onion is translucent, 4 to 5 minutes. Add quinoa; cook, stirring occasionally, for 30 seconds. Add water; increase heat to high and bring to a boil. Reduce heat to medium; cover and cook for 15 minutes. Remove from heat; let stand, covered, for 5 minutes. Stir in chicken, marinara, Parmesan and 1/2 cup basil.

2. Trim top 1/2 inch from peppers; remove seeds and membranes. Arrange the peppers, cut-sides up, in an 8-inch-square glass baking dish. Cover with plastic wrap; microwave on High for 3 minutes. Remove plastic wrap. Spoon the quinoa mixture

evenly into the pepper halves (about 1 1/4 cups each).

3. Bake the stuffed peppers until they are softened, about 15 minutes. Sprinkle evenly with mozzarella. Continue baking until the cheese is melted, 5 to 7 minutes. Sprinkle evenly with the remaining 1/4 cup basil.

Tips

To make ahead: The peppers can be prepared through Step 2 up to 1 day in advance. Cover and refrigerate. Let stand at room temperature while preheating the oven. Continue with Step 3.

Nutrition Facts:

Calories 559 Total Carbohydrate 49g Dietary Fiber 8g Total Sugars 13g Protein 48g Total Fat 18g Saturated Fat 5g Cholesterol 104mg Vitamin A 5915iu Vitamin C 218mg Folate 173mcg Sodium 522mg Calcium 245mg Iron 5mg Magnesium 149mg Potassium 969mg

Instant Pot Thai Coconut Lime Chicken Soup with Noodles

Cooking Time: 29 Mins.

Servings: 6

Ingredients:

- Thai Whole Chicken
- 2.5 lb. whole chicken
- 2 inch piece of fresh ginger, sliced in matchsticks
- 8 cloves garlic, smashed
- 1 medium onion, cut into quarters
- 2 small thai red chilis or jalapeno
- 1 handful cilantro stems
- 1 cup chicken broth or water
- 1 tsp coarse sea salt
- 1/2 tsp fresh ground black pepper
- Coconut Lime Broth
- 2 cans coconut milk *I used 1 full-fat and 1 lite
- 2 tsp freshly grated ginger
- 1 medium thai red chili, sliced or jalapeno
- 1 lime
- 1 tsp sea salt
- Add-In's
- 4 cups swiss chard or other leafy green like spinach or kale

- 8 ounces noodles *see notes for options*
- Toppings
- fresh sliced chili
- fresh cilantro leaves
- lime wedge

Directions:

1. Remove the bag of giblets from inside the cavity of the chicken (if the chicken came with them). Wash the chicken well and dry with paper towels.
2. Add chicken to the insert of your instant pot, sprinkle with salt and pepper and cover with ginger, garlic, onion, chilis, cilantro stems, and chicken broth.
3. Carefully place the lid on instant pot and turn to locked position. Once the lid is locked turn the vent to the "sealing" position.
4. Select the manual setting to 25 minutes. After 25 minutes allow the pressure to naturally release for 10 minutes, then turn the vent valve to "venting" and carefully allow the remainder of the pressure to release.
5. Carefully remove the chicken from the broth. It should be fall off the bone tender. Set aside.
6. Thai Coconut Lime Broth
7. Using a fine mesh sieve strain the broth over a large bowl. Return the broth to the instant pot. Add coconut milk through sea salt (all ingredients from teh broth section). Stir well to combine.
8. Replace the lid and lock in place. Turn the vent to "sealing" position. Press the manual button and set to 3 minutes.
9. While broth is getting all fragrant and perfect, shred your chicken and set aside.
10. Cook noodles according to package instructions (see notes on why I don't do this step in the instant pot)
11. After 3 minutes allow broth to natural release for a few minutes and then gently turn the vent valve to the "venting" position and carefully manually release the pressure.
12. Remove lid, add swiss chard to the hot broth and stir until gently wilted (about 1 or 2 minutes)
13. Plating
14. Ladle broth into bowls, add shredded chicken, noodles, fresh cilantro, sliced chilis (optional), and an additional squeeze of lime juice.

Notes

I make the noodles separately because I don't like soggy noodles and I haven't found an instant pot recipe that produces al dente noodles yet. If you have one, send it to me!

I used a Korean noodle in this dish because I am all about fusion ;-) Or because a new Korean market opened in my neighborhood and I had to buy all the new things! You can use angel hair pasta or really any noodle that you like

I have never tried this with chicken breast, but I imagine it would work. To be totally frank, I find that chicken breast does not come out well in the instant pot and I personally love using a whole chicken.

Nutrition facts are for the whole chicken, as I mentioned in the instructions you will have quite a lot of chicken meat and may want to reserve half for another recipe.

Nutrition Facts:

Calories: 846kcal | Carbohydrates: 34g | Protein: 55g | Fat: 54g | Saturated Fat: 24g | Cholesterol: 198mg | Sodium: 1195mg | Potassium: 727mg | Fiber: 1g | Sugar: 3g | Vitamin A: 1840IU | Vitamin C: 17.4mg | Calcium: 55mg | Iron: 3.5mg

Instant Pot Apricot Ginger Chicken Thighs with Bok Choy

Cooking Time: 15 Mins.

Servings: 2

Ingredients:

- 1 lb. boneless, skinless chicken thighs
- 12 ounces baby bok choy about 6-8 small heads
- 1/2 cup apricot jam (I used low sugar apricot jam)
- 1/4 cup coconut aminos or soy sauce
- 2 tsp fresh turmeric, grated or 1 tsp dried ground turmeric
- 6 cloves garlic, crushed
- 1 tbsp fresh ginger, grated
- 1/4 tsp black pepper

Directions:

1. Prepare the sauce by whisking together coconut aminos (or soy sauce), apricot jam, garlic, ginger, and turmeric.
2. Set Instant Pot to saute, pour the sauce in and cook for 2 minutes stirring occasionally (you are just reducing the sauce a bit before you cook the chicken). Turn off the saute function.
3. Add the chicken to the Instant pot and dredge in the sauce. Close the lid and place the valve in the

SEALING position. Set on manual for 10 minutes.

4. Once the chicken is done, perform a quick release. Remove the chicken from the pot.

5. Add the steamer insert to the pot (handles up) and place the bok choy on top of the basket. Replace the instant pot lid, place the valve in the SEALING position and set on manual for 1 minute. When finished perform a quick release.

6. Remove the bok choy and carefully remove the steamer insert.

7. Reduce the sauce: Press the saute button and stir the sauce until it has reduced by half. It should be thicker and stickier.

8. Serve over white or brown rice or cauliflower rice, drizzle sauce on top of the chicken and the steamed bok choy.

Nutrition Facts:

Serving: 1serving | Calories: 481kcal | Carbohydrates: 51g | Protein: 46g | Fat: 10g | Saturated Fat: 2g | Cholesterol: 215mg | Sodium: 1016mg | Potassium: 637mg | Fiber: 2g | Sugar: 28g | Vitamin A: 7745IU | Vitamin C: 85mg | Calcium: 236mg | Iron: 3mg

BREAKFAST AND BRUNCH RECIPES

Artichoke Ricotta Flatbread.

Cooking Time: 10 Mins.

Servings: 4

Ingredients:

- 1/2 pound homemade or store bought pizza dough at room temperature
- olive oil for drizzling
- 1 1/2 cups fresh whole milk ricotta cheese
- 2 tablespoons fresh basil chopped + more for serving
- 1 tablespoon honey + more fore serving if desired
- 8 ounces marinated artichokes drained
- 6 ounces fresh mortadella or prosciutto torn (omit if vegetarian)
- 3 cups fresh arugula
- 1/2 cup fresh shaved parmesan cheese
- 1 tablespoon fresh chives chopped
- crushed red pepper flakes for sprinkling (if desired)
- Lemon Vinaigrette
- 1/3 cup olive oil
- juice + zest of 1 lemon
- 2 teaspoons apple cider vinegar
- salt to taste

Directions:

1. Preheat the oven to 450 degrees F. Grease a large baking sheet with olive oil.
2. On a lightly floured surface, push/roll the dough out until until it is very thin. Transfer the dough to the prepared baking sheet and drizzle with olive oil + sprinkle lightly with salt + pepper. Place in the oven and bake for 8-10 minutes or until the crust is golden.
3. Meanwhile, stir together the ricotta, basil, honey and a pinch of both salt and pepper. Remove the bread from the oven and top with the ricotta. Scatter on the artichokes and then sprinkle with crushed red pepper flakes, if desired. Add the torn mortadella or prosciutto. Top with fresh arugula and shaved parmesan. Just before serving drizzle with the lemon vinaigrette and chives. EAT!
4. Lemon Vinaigrette
5. In a small bowl, whisk together all of the ingredients, add salt to taste. Drizzle over the flatbread.

Nutrition Facts:

Calories: 826kcal | Carbohydrates: 41g | Protein: 27g | Fat: 58g | Saturated Fat: 18g | Cholesterol: 79mg | Sodium: 997mg | Potassium: 270mg | Fiber: 2g | Sugar: 9g | Vitamin A: 1535IU | Vitamin C: 28.9mg | Calcium: 389mg | Iron: 3.5mg

Walnut Sage Pesto Pasta with Roasted Delicata Squash

Cooking Time: 30 Minutes

Servings: 4 – 6

Ingredients:

- Roasted Delicata Squash:
- 2 medium delicata squash scrubbed and rinsed well
- 2 tablespoons (30 mL) extra virgin olive oil
- kosher salt
- freshly ground black pepper
- Walnut Sage Pesto:
- 1 packed cup flat-leaf parsley leaves
- ¾ cup toasted or raw walnut halves if you're not using roasted walnut oil, I recommend toasting the walnuts for best flavor
- 2-3 medium garlic cloves
- 6-7 fresh, large sage leaves
- ½ (120 mL) cup roasted walnut oil I recommend La Tourangelle brand
- kosher salt
- freshly ground black pepper
- For the Pasta and Serving:
- fresh sage leaves, for frying I like to garnish each serving with 3-4 leaves
- roughly ¼ cup extra virgin olive oil
- 1 lb dried whole wheat penne or fusilli
- ½ cup finely grated parmigiano-reggiano cheese plus more for serving

Directions:

1. Preheat the oven to 425°F (218°C). Line a sheet pan with aluminum foil or parchment paper. Set aside. Meanwhile, bring a large pot of salted water to a boil for the pasta.

2. Trim the ends of the delicata squash and slice them in half lengthwise. Using a spoon, scoop out and discard the seeds. Cut each squash half into ½-inch thick half-moon slices and place on the sheet pan. Drizzle with olive oil, salt, and pepper, and spread them evenly on the sheet pan so they are not touching. Roast for 20 to 25 minutes, flipping the squash halfway through, until they are tender and caramelized.

3. As the squash is roasting, prepare the walnut-sage pesto. Combine the parsley leaves, walnuts, garlic

cloves, and fresh sage leaves in the bowl of a large food processor, fitted with a blade attachment, and pulse until coarsely chopped. Add the roasted walnut oil and process until mostly smooth. Season to taste with salt and pepper, and transfer to a bowl. If you wish, you can add a touch of fresh lemon juice or zest too.

4. Line a small plate with paper towels. In a small non-stick pan, heat a thin layer of extra virgin olive oil (about ¼ cup) over medium-high heat until hot. Fry the sage leaves, in batches, until crisp (it should only take a few seconds). Transfer with a slotted spoon to the plate and season lightly with salt. Set aside for serving.

5. As the squash finishes roasting, add the dried whole wheat pasta to the boiling water and cook until al dente. Reserve roughly 1 cup (240 mL) of the starchy pasta cooking water and drain the pasta. Transfer the pasta back to the same pot, drizzle lightly with olive oil, and add the walnut-sage pesto and grated parmigiano-reggiano cheese. Toss until the pasta is evenly coated in the sauce, adding some of the reserved pasta water as needed (this amount of pesto will generously coat all of the pasta, but the starchy cooking water will help create an even creamier, better distributed sauce.

6. Serve topped with roasted Delicata squash pieces and fried sage leaves. Top with grated parmigiano-reggiano cheese (as desired).

Tips for Success:

If cannot find or do not wish to purchase roasted walnut oil for this recipe, you can substitute it with extra virgin olive oil. However, if this is the case, I highly recommend toasting the walnut halves to account for the missing flavor!

Whenever I make pesto, I prefer to prepare the pesto without the cheese (this is best practice if you want to prepare the pesto ahead of time or if you are freezing an extra batch too!) and just add the freshly grated cheese as I'm tossing the pasta with the sauce.

Best Asian Garlic Paleo Whole30 Noodles

Servings: 4

Ingredients:

Noodles

- 1 large cooked spaghetti squashsee notes on how to cook
- 1/2 medium zucchinijulienne cut
- 1/2 large carrotjulienne cut

- 1 small red bell pepperminced
- 1/2 cup fresh cilantrodiced
- 1/4 cup roasted cashewsor peanuts- chopped

Sauce

- 2/3 cup coconut aminos
- 1/4 cup full fat coconut milk
- 2 tablespoons fresh grated gingeror powder
- 2 tablespoons red curry paste
- 2 tablespoons fish sauce
- 6 medium/large garlic clovessmaller cloves for less spicy
- 6 large medjool datespitted

Directions:

1. Puree ingredients for sauce in a blender.
2. In a large bowl incorporate ingredients for noodles, pour sauce in, and mix together. Serve recipe hot or cold. Personally, I like it best served as is- chilled. If you want to heat the noodles, just mix everything together in a skillet and heat until warm.

Recipe Notes

How to bake spaghetti squash: cut spaghetti squash in half lengthwise, use a large spoon to scrape the seeds from the center, lay face up on a baking tray, and brush lightly with olive oil. Bake on 450F for 25 minutes (cook longer for softer noodles).

Spaghetti Squash with Asparagus, Ricotta, Lemon, and Thyme

Servings: 2 to 4

Ingredients:

- 1 small spaghetti squash (about 1 1/2 pounds)
- 1 tablespoon olive oil, divided
- 2 cloves garlic, smashed
- 1 pound asparagus
- 3/4 cup ricotta cheese
- 3 tablespoons freshly squeezed lemon juice (from about 1 medium lemon)
- 1 teaspoon finely grated lemon zest
- 1 teaspoon fresh thyme leaves (from 4 to 5 sprigs)
- 1/2 teaspoon kosher salt
- 1/4 teaspoon freshly ground black pepper
- 3 tablespoons pine nuts, toasted

Directions:

1. Arrange a rack in the middle of the oven and heat to 375°F.
2. Cut the squash in half lengthwise and scrape out the seeds. Brush the cut sides with 1/2 tablespoon of the oil. Place cut-side down on one half of a rimmed baking sheet. Roast for 35 minutes. Meanwhile, trim the woody ends of the asparagus and cut the

stalks on a diagonal into 2-inch pieces.

3. Remove the baking sheet with the squash, add the asparagus to the other side, and toss with the remaining 1/2 tablespoon oil. Place a garlic clove beneath each squash half. Return the baking sheet to the oven and roast until the asparagus is tender and starting to char, and the squash is easily pierced with a fork, about 10 minutes. Meanwhile, place the ricotta, lemon juice, zest, thyme, salt, and pepper in a large bowl, and stir to combine.

4. Remove the baking sheet from the oven and carefully remove the garlic cloves from beneath the squash. Add to the ricotta and mix well. Add the asparagus to the bowl.

5. When the squash is cool enough to handle but still warm, run a fork through the flesh to separate and remove the strands from the shell. Add to the ricotta mixture and stir to combine. Divide between plates or transfer to a serving platter and top with the pine nuts.

Recipe Notes

Storage: Leftovers can be stored in a covered container in the refrigerator for up to 4 days.

Turmeric Milk

Cooking Time: 5 Mins.

Servings: 1

Ingredients:

- 1 (1 1/2 inch) piece fresh turmeric root, peeled and grated
- 1 (1/2 inch) piece fresh ginger root, peeled and grated
- 1 tablespoon honey
- 1 cup unsweetened almond milk
- 1 pinch ground turmeric
- 1 pinch ground cinnamon

Directions:

1. Combine turmeric root, ginger root, and honey together in a bowl, crushing the turmeric and ginger as much as possible.

2. Heat almond milk in a saucepan over medium-low heat. Once small bubbles begin to form around the edges, reduce heat to low. Transfer about 2 tablespoon milk to turmeric mixture to allow mixture to soften and honey to melt into a paste-like mixture.

3. Mix the turmeric paste into milk in the saucepan; raise temperature to medium-low and cook, stirring continuously, until fully combined. Blend

with an immersion blender for a smooth texture.
4. Pour turmeric tea into a mug and top with ground turmeric and cinnamon.
5. Cook's Notes:
6. Pregnant or nursing women, young children, or diabetics should consult their physician before consuming turmeric.
7. Turmeric can stain any utensil, working area, or skin.
8. Any milk or milk substitute will do here. Agave nectar can be used in place of honey.

Nutrition Facts:

Calories 143 Total Fat 3g Saturated Fat 0g Sodium 163mg Total Carbohydrate 29g Dietary Fiber 2g Total Sugars 25g Protein 2g Vitamin C 1mg Calcium 228mg Iron 1mg Potassium 279mg

Protein Overnight Oats

Cooking Time: 4 Hours

Servings: 1

Ingredients:

- ¼ cup old-fashioned rolled oats
- 1 tablespoon chia seeds
- 3 tablespoons whole unsweetened Greek yogurt traditional or plant-based for vegan and dairy-free diet
- 2 teaspoons maple syrup
- ¼ teaspoon pure vanilla extract
- ½ cup almond milk or milk of choice
- 1 scoop vanilla protein powder of choice
- Optional Toppings
- chopped fruit, sliced banana, nuts, seeds, nut butter, flaked coconut

Directions:

1. To a 8-oz mason jar, add the oats, chia seeds, yogurt, maple syrup, vanilla extract, almond milk and protein powder.
2. Cover and shake until the ingredients are very well mixed. Let settle for 2-3 minutes, then shake again until you see no clumping.
3. Store in the fridge overnight or at least 4 hours.
4. When ready to serve, uncover and add any topping you like.
5. Store, refrigerated, for up to 4 days.

Notes

Rolled oats work best for this recipe. Steel cut oats will not work.

Nutrition Facts:

Serving: 1 (of 1) | Calories: 306kcal | Carbohydrates: 27g | Protein: 29g | Fat: 7g | Saturated Fat: 1g |

Polyunsaturated Fat: 4g | Monounsaturated Fat: 1g | Cholesterol: 64mg | Sodium: 260mg | Potassium: 342mg | Fiber: 7g | Sugar: 8g | Vitamin A: 8IU | Vitamin C: 0.2mg | Calcium: 455mg | Iron: 2mg

Sweet Potato Hashbrown Egg Nests

Servings: 12

Ingredients:

- 2 medium russet potatoes scrubbed clean
- 2 medium sweet potatoes scrubbed clean
- 3 tablespoons olive oil plus more for greasing the muffin tin
- ¼ teaspoon kosher salt plus more for sprinkling
- 12 large eggs

Directions:

1. Preheat the oven to 400 degrees.
2. Bake the russet and sweet potatoes until they're cooked through but not quite tender, about 20 minutes. The goal is just to pre-bake them a bit, so they should still be pretty firm.
3. Let the potatoes cool enough to handle, then peel and grate, using the largest grating size.
4. In a large bowl, toss the grated potatoes, olive oil, and salt.
5. Grease the muffin tin with olive oil.
6. Add the grated potato mixture to a 12-cup muffin pan, 1/3 cup at a time. The mixture will shrink significantly when baked, so it's okay if there's a lot of mixture in each cup. If you end up with extra potato mixture, feel free to use it to make additional egg cups.
7. Use your fingers to lightly press the center of each cup so the potatoes spill over the top a bit.
8. Increase the oven temperature to 425 degrees, then bake until the potatoes are golden brown, about 20-25 minutes. Keep on eye on them so the ends of the potato shreds don't burn.
9. Remove from the oven, let the nests cool a bit, then crack one egg into each cup and sprinkle with additional kosher salt to taste.
10. Return to the oven and bake for 10-15 minutes, depending on how cooked you like your eggs. Let cool slightly, then serve immediately.

Notes

If you're making these ahead of time, prepare the recipe through step seven. When ready to serve, add the eggs and proceed with the recipe.

The egg nests can also be fully made ahead of time and gently reheated in a 350F oven or on the stovetop.

DIY Greek Quinoa Bowl

Servings: 4

Ingredients:

- For the Bowls
- 1 cup quinoa rinsed and drained
- ½ teaspoon salt
- 1 15- oz can chickpeas or 2 cup cooked lentils or white beans
- 1 English cucumber thinly sliced
- 1-2 bell peppers red, orange, or yellow, thinly sliced
- 1 pint cherry tomatoes
- 4 cups baby spinach
- For the Tahini Dressing
- ¼ cup tahini sesame seed paste
- 1 clove garlic very finely minced or grated
- ½ cup red wine vinegar
- ¼ teaspoon salt
- ¼ teaspoon dried oregano
- 1 teaspoon honey
- 1/3 cup warm water

Directions:

1. Place the rinsed, drained quinoa in a medium saucepan. Add 2 cups of water and the salt. Cover, bring to a boil, then reduce to a simmer. Simmer, covered, for 18 minutes. Turn off the heat and let sit for an additional 5 minutes. Uncover and fluff with a fork.
2. Add the rinsed, drained chickpeas and stir to warm through.
3. In a medium bowl or jar, whisk or shake together the tahini, garlic, vinegar, salt, oregano, honey and water until very well combined.
4. Assemble by dividing the spinach, quinoa/chickpea mixture, cucumber, bell peppers, and tomatoes in bowls. Drizzle with the Tahini Dressing and serve.

Notes

Serve all the parts of the bowl (quinoa, chickpeas, veggies) separately on a plate with the Tahini Dressing on the side for dipping.

Add simply grilled chicken or shrimp to bump up the protein.

Use white beans in place of the chickpeas, brown rice in place of the quinoa, and any mix of veggies you like. These are DIY bowls, so feel free to use what you like and what you have on hand!

Slow Cooker Enchilada Quinoa

Cooking Time: 3 Hours

Servings: 6

Ingredients:

- 1 small yellow onion finely chopped
- 1 red bell pepper finely chopped
- 1 teaspoon ground cumin
- 1 teaspoon garlic powder
- 1 teaspoon mild chili powder
- 2 (15-oz) cans black beans drained and rinsed
- 1 (15-oz) can tomato sauce
- 1 (15-oz) can diced fire-roasted tomatoes
- 1 cup water
- 1-3 teaspoons salt
- 1 cup uncooked quinoa rinsed
- 1 (4-oz) can chopped green chilies
- Juice of 1 small lime
- Optional Toppings
- Easy Guacamole
- Fresh Tomato Salsa

Directions:

1. Combine the onion, bell pepper, cumin, garlic powder, chili powder, beans, tomato sauce, fire-roasted tomatoes, water, salt (taste the mixture prior to adding the quinoa, adding salt to taste), and quinoa to a 6-quart slow cooker, stirring to combine. Cover and cook on high for 3 hours or on low for 6 hours, or until the quinoa is cooked through.
2. Uncover and stir in the green chilies and lime juice. Taste and add additional salt or lime juice if you like.
3. Serve with any toppings you like such as avocado, chopped green onions, cilantro, grated cheese, sour cream, hot sauce, or sliced limes. If you want crunch, go for crushed corn chips and chopped white onion.

Notes

Pull aside a portion prior to adding the green chilis if you're serving someone sensitive to heat.

Top with avocado and chopped green onions, or sprinkle with cheese and dollop with sour cream.

Since the consistency of this dish is decidedly creamy, feel free to top with crushed corn chips or chopped white onion to add crunch.

Nutrition Facts:

Serving: 1 (of 6) | Calories: 231kcal | Carbohydrates: 44g | Protein: 11g | Fat: 2g | Saturated Fat: 0.3g | Polyunsaturated Fat: 1g | Monounsaturated Fat: 1g | Sodium: 1252mg | Potassium: 861mg | Fiber: 11g | Sugar: 7g | Vitamin A: 1147IU | Vitamin C: 44mg | Calcium: 87mg | Iron: 5mg

Spinach & Artichoke Dip Pasta

Servings: 4

Ingredients:

- 8 ounces whole-wheat rotini
- 1 (5 ounce) package baby spinach, roughly chopped
- 4 ounces reduced-fat cream cheese, cut into chunks
- ¾ cup reduced-fat milk
- ½ cup grated Parmesan cheese, plus more for garnish, if desired
- 2 teaspoons garlic powder
- ¼ teaspoon ground pepper
- 1 (14 ounce) can artichoke hearts, rinsed, squeezed dry and chopped (see Tip)

Directions:

1. Bring a large saucepan of water to a boil. Cook pasta according to package directions. Drain.
2. Combine spinach and 1 tablespoon water in a large saucepan over medium heat. Cook, stirring occasionally, until just wilted, about 2 minutes. Transfer to a small bowl.
3. Add cream cheese and milk to the pan; whisk until the cream cheese is melted.
4. Add Parmesan, garlic powder and pepper; cook, whisking until thickened and bubbling.
5. Drain as much liquid as possible from the spinach. Stir the drained spinach into the sauce, along with artichokes and the pasta. Cook until warmed through.

Tip

If you can find frozen artichoke hearts, they also work well in this recipe. Thaw before using.

Nutrition Facts:

Calories 371 Total Carbohydrate 56g Dietary Fiber 8g Total Sugars 6g Protein 17g Total Fat 9g Saturated Fat 4g Cholesterol 26mg Vitamin A 2827iu Vitamin C 17mg Folate 9mcg Sodium 550mg Calcium 240mg Iron 3mg Magnesium 37mg Potassium 397mg

20-Minute Balsamic Mushroom & Spinach Pasta

Servings: 6

Ingredients:

- 8 ounces whole-wheat fettuccine or linguine
- 4 tablespoons extra-virgin olive oil, divided
- 1 pound cremini mushrooms, sliced (about 6 cups)
- 1 ½ tablespoons thinly sliced garlic
- 3 ounces baby spinach (about 3 cups)
- 3 tablespoons balsamic vinegar
- 2 teaspoons Worcestershire sauce, preferably

vegetarian

- ¾ teaspoon salt
- ½ teaspoon ground pepper
- ¼ cup chopped fresh basil
- 6 tablespoons chopped roasted unsalted pistachios

Directions:

1. Bring a large pot of water to a boil. Cook pasta according to package directions. Drain, reserving 1/4 cup cooking water.
2. Meanwhile, heat 2 tablespoons oil in a large nonstick skillet over medium-high heat. Add mushrooms; cook, stirring occasionally, until well-browned, about 10 minutes. Stir in garlic; cook, stirring constantly, until fragrant, about 30 seconds. Stir in spinach; cook, stirring constantly, until wilted, about 1 minute.
3. Reduce heat to medium-low; stir in balsamic vinegar, Worcestershire, salt, pepper and the remaining 2 tablespoons oil. Add the pasta and toss to coat. Stir in the reserved 1/4 cup cooking water. Remove from heat. Stir in basil and sprinkle with pistachios.

Nutrition Facts:

Calories 276 Total Carbohydrate 35g Dietary Fiber 5g Total Sugars 5g Protein 10g Total Fat 14g Saturated Fat 2g Vitamin A 1034iu Sodium 332mg Potassium 457mg

Creamy Spinach Pasta

Servings: 4

Ingredients:

- 12 ounces uncooked tube-shaped chickpea pasta (about 3 1/2 cups) (such as Banza)
- 1 clove garlic, thinly sliced (about 1 tsp.)
- 2 tablespoons thinly sliced shallots
- 3 ¼ ounces mascarpone cheese
- 4 ounces fresh baby spinach
- 1 teaspoon kosher salt
- ½ teaspoon black pepper
- 1 teaspoon lemon zest (from 1 lemon)
- 1 pinch Crushed red pepper

Directions:

1. Cook pasta according to package directions, omitting salt. Drain, reserving 1 cup cooking water.
2. Transfer pasta to a large bowl; add garlic, shallot, mascarpone, spinach, salt, pepper, and 1/2 cup of the reserved cooking liquid. Stir until cheese has melted and mixture is combined, about 1 1/2 minutes. Add additional cooking liquid as needed to loosen sauce. Divide pasta among 4 bowls.

Sprinkle with lemon zest and, if desired, crushed red pepper. Serve immediately.

Nutrition Facts:

Calories 395 Total Carbohydrate 50g Dietary Fiber 13g Total Sugars 8g Protein 23g Total Fat 16g Saturated Fat 6g Sodium 604mg

Spinach, Lima Bean & Crispy Pancetta Pasta

Servings: 4

Ingredients:

- 1 (9 ounce) package fresh spinach pasta
- 1 tablespoon extra-virgin olive oil
- 4 ounces diced pancetta
- 1 (16 ounce) package frozen baby lima beans, thawed
- 1 cup sliced shallots
- 2 cloves garlic, minced
- ½ teaspoon dried rosemary
- 4 cups baby spinach
- 3 tablespoons lemon juice
- ¾ cup grated pecorino cheese, divided

Directions:

1. Bring a medium saucepan of water to a boil over high heat. Add pasta and cook according to package directions. Reserve 1 cup of water, then drain the pasta.

2. Meanwhile, heat oil in a large skillet over medium-high heat. Add pancetta and cook, stirring occasionally, until crispy, 6 to 8 minutes. Remove with a slotted spoon to a plate. Add lima beans and shallots to the pan. Cook, stirring occasionally, until the shallots are tender, about 3 minutes. Stir in garlic and rosemary; cook, stirring, until fragrant, about 1 minute. Add spinach and cook until wilted, about 2 minutes.

3. Add the pasta and the reserved water to the pan. Cook, stirring, until the sauce is thickened, about 1 minute. Stir in lemon juice, the pancetta and half the pecorino. Serve the pasta topped with the remaining pecorino.

Nutrition Facts:

Calories 477 Total Carbohydrate 62g Dietary Fiber 8g Total Sugars 3g Protein 21g Total Fat 16g Saturated Fat 7g Cholesterol 74mg Vitamin A 4439iu Vitamin C 29mg Folate 197mcg Sodium 687mg Calcium 124mg Iron 6mg Magnesium 136mg Potassium 663mg

Spicy Cauliflower Burrito Bowl

Cooking Time: 30 Mins.

Servings: 4

Ingredients:

- 1 large head of cauliflower about 3-4 cups of cauliflower florets
- 1 large red bell pepper sliced
- 1 large red onion sliced
- 2 tbsp avocado oil
- 1 tsp garlic powder
- 1 tsp chili powder
- 1/4 tsp sea salt
- 2 cups cooked quinoa
- 2 cups black beans
- 1/4 cup fresh cilantro, chopped
- 1/4 cup lime juice
- Toppings
- fresh sliced jalapeno
- guacamole
- fresh cilantro
- lime wedges

Directions:

1. ROAST VEGGIES
2. On a large sheet pan toss cauliflower, red bell pepper, and red onion with avocado oil, dried spices and salt. Place in a 350° oven for 25-35 minutes until tender. Remove from oven and set aside.
3. QUINOA
4. Cook quinoa according to instructions (I typically use 1/4 cup less water for a drier quinoa - I personally hate quinoa mush).
5. Once quinoa is cooked toss with black beans, cilantro, lime juice, and salt to taste.
6. BUILD YOUR BURRITO BOWL
7. Start with a layer of quinoa/ black bean mixture. Top with cauliflower, red peppers and onions, and a generous scoop of guacamole. Add sliced jalapeno, fresh cilatnro, and a squeeze of lime juice.
8. Store ingredients in separate containers in the refrigerator for up to 5 days.

Notes

*Nutrition Analysis is an estimate and is estimated without the guacamole *

INGREDIENTS YOU CAN ADD TO A BURRITO BOWL:

This is in no way a comprehensive list, but as you can see... your options are kind of endless!

Switch up the grain - quinoa, rice, farro, or barley!

Pick a bean - chickpeas, black beans, kidney beans, you get the idea

Add toppings:

Corn

Tomatoes

Salsa

Pico de Gallo

Avocado - Gahhhh!

Guacamole - DOUBLE Gahhhhhh!! Absolutely use my recipe for healthy guacamole, it is without a doubt the best guac!

Sour Cream

Shredded Cheese

Roasted Zucchini

and on, and on, and on.

Nutrition Facts:

Serving: 1serving | Calories: 371kcal | Carbohydrates: 58g | Protein: 17g | Fat: 10g | Saturated Fat: 1g | Sodium: 228mg | Potassium: 1255mg | Fiber: 16g | Sugar: 8g | Vitamin A: 1499IU | Vitamin C: 160mg | Calcium: 94mg | Iron: 4mg

Strawberry-Chia Breakfast Pudding

Servings: 4

Ingredients:

- .50 cup chia seeds
- ⅛ teaspoon kosher salt
- .50 cup plain whole-milk yogurt or unsweetened coconut yogurt
- 1 teaspoon pure vanilla extract
- 2 cups whole milk or coconut milk
- 1 pound fresh strawberries, hulled and thinly sliced (4 cups), plus more for serving
- 3 tablespoons granulated sugar
- .50 cup granola

Directions:

1. Combine chia seeds and salt in a medium bowl. Whisk in yogurt and vanilla. Slowly pour in milk, whisking constantly. Continue to whisk for 1 minute to break up any clumps. Cover and refrigerate for at least 4 hours and up to overnight.
2. Gently toss strawberries with sugar in a bowl. Cover and refrigerate for at least 1 hour and up to overnight.
3. To serve, divide strawberry mixture between 4 glasses or bowls, using a slotted spoon. Top with chia pudding, 2 tablespoons granola each, and

more sliced strawberries.

Berry Baked Oatmeal

Servings: 8

Ingredients:

- 3 large eggs
- 3 ½ cups whole milk
- ¼ cup pure maple syrup, plus more for serving
- 2 teaspoons pure vanilla extract
- ½ teaspoon ground nutmeg
- ¼ cup (1/2 stick) unsalted butter, melted and cooled, divided, plus more for greasing
- 4 cups old-fashioned rolled oats
- 2 teaspoons baking powder
- 1 teaspoon kosher salt
- 2 cups mixed berries, sliced if strawberries
- ½ cup sliced almonds, lightly toasted

Directions:

1. Preheat oven to 400°F. Grease a 13-by-9-inch baking dish with butter. Whisk eggs, milk, syrup, vanilla, nutmeg, and 2 tablespoons melted butter in a large bowl. Add oats, baking powder, and salt; stir to combine. Transfer to baking dish; spread in a mostly even layer using a spatula. Top with berries and almonds.

2. Bake until lightly golden and firm in center, 40 to 45 minutes. Let rest for 10 minutes. Drizzle or brush with remaining 2 tablespoons melted butter. Serve with more syrup.

Savory Oatmeal With Spinach and Poached Eggs

Servings: 4

Ingredients:

- 2 tablespoons olive oil
- ½ medium yellow onion, chopped
- 1 cup old-fashioned rolled oats
- 2 cups water
- 4 ounces Parmesan cheese, grated (about 1 cup), divided
- 1 ¾ teaspoons kosher salt, divided
- 1 ¼ teaspoons black pepper, divided
- 2 cups baby spinach (about 2 oz.)
- 4 large eggs, poached
- 2 tablespoons chopped fresh chives

Directions:

1. Heat oil in a medium skillet over medium-high. Add onion and cook, stirring occasionally, until tender, 3 to 4 minutes. Stir in oats; cook 1 minute. Add water and bring to a boil. Reduce heat to

medium, and simmer, stirring often, until oats are tender, about 8 minutes. Remove from heat.

2. Stir ¾ cup cheese, ¾ teaspoon salt, and ¼ teaspoon pepper into oats mixture. Spoon ½ cup of oats mixture into each of 4 serving bowls; top each with ½ cup spinach and 1 poached egg. Sprinkle evenly with remaining 1 teaspoon each salt and pepper, and top evenly with remaining ¼ cup cheese. Sprinkle evenly with chives.

Nutrition Facts:

Calories 346   Total Fat 21g   Saturated Fat 7g   Cholesterol 210mg   Sodium 1446mg   Total Carbohydrate 22g   Total Sugars 2g   Protein 18g

Easy Sheet-Pan Dinner: Shawarma-Seasoned Cauliflower and Chickpea Pitas

Servings: 4

Ingredients:

- 1 1/2-lb head cauliflower, cut into medium florets
- 15-oz can chickpeas, drained and rinsed
- 3 Tbsp olive oil
- 1 Tbsp shawarma spice blend
- 1 1/4 tsp kosher salt
- 1/4 cup coarsely chopped fresh mint, plus leaves for serving
- 3/4 cup plain whole-milk yogurt
- 4 6 1/2-inch pita rounds, warmed
- 2 Persian cucumbers, sliced into half-moons
- 1/4 cup thinly sliced red onion

Directions:

1. Preheat oven to 450°F. Toss cauliflower florets, chickpeas, oil, shawarma spice blend, and salt on a large rimmed baking sheet. Spread in an even layer.
2. Roast until cauliflower is tender and golden brown, about 30 minutes, stirring halfway through. Let cool slightly, about 5 minutes. Stir in chopped mint.
3. Spread 3 tablespoons yogurt on each pita. Top pitas with cauliflower-chickpea mixture, cucumbers, and onion. Top with mint leaves.
4. Preheat air fryer to 400°F for 2 minutes. Working in batches if necessary, place the cauliflower-chickpea mixture in a single layer in air fryer basket. Cook until cauliflower is tender and beginning to brown, about 15 minutes, stirring halfway through. Transfer to a heatproof bowl. Let cool slightly before adding mint and proceeding with step 3.

Nutrition Facts:

Calories 607   Total Fat 17g   Saturated Fat 3g   Cholesterol 8mg   Sodium 1378mg   Total

Carbohydrate 94g   Dietary Fiber 15g   Total Sugars 14g   Protein 24g   Vitamin C 81mg   Calcium 236mg   Iron 7mg   Potassium 914mg

Avocado Grain Bowl With Beet Ginger Dressing

Servings: 4

Ingredients:

- ½ cup red rice or short-grain brown rice
- 2 ¼ teaspoons kosher salt, divided
- ½ cup dried brown lentils, rinsed
- ½ cup rainbow quinoa
- ¼ cup olive oil, divided, plus more for serving
- ¼ cup plain whole-milk kefir
- 1 8.8-oz. pkg. steamed beets (such as Love Beets), chopped (1¾ cups)
- 1 tablespoon fresh lemon juice (from 1 lemon)
- 1 teaspoon grated fresh ginger (from a 1-in. piece)
- 2 avocados, halved, pitted, and peeled
- 1 small bulb fennel, thinly sliced
- ¼ cup hemp seeds
- baby greens, flaky sea salt, and crushed red pepper, for serving

Directions:

1. Place 3½ cups water, rice, and 1 teaspoon kosher salt in a medium saucepan. Bring to a boil over medium-high. Reduce heat to medium-low; cover and simmer for 25 minutes.
2. Stir in lentils; cover and cook for 10 minutes.
3. Stir in quinoa; cover and cook until grains are tender and all water is absorbed, 12 to 15 minutes.
4. Remove lid, cover pan with a clean dish towel, and replace lid. Let stand for 10 minutes.
5. Spread grains on a rimmed baking sheet and let cool for 10 minutes. Toss grains with 3 tablespoons oil and ½ teaspoon kosher salt on baking sheet. (Grains can be made up to 3 days ahead; store in an airtight container in the refrigerator.)
6. Meanwhile, place kefir, beets, lemon juice, ginger, and remaining ¾ teaspoon kosher salt and 1 tablespoon oil in a blender. Process until smooth, about 30 seconds.
7. Spoon beet mixture on 1 side of each plate and spread with back of a spoon into a half-moon shape.
8. Top with grains mixture, avocado, fennel, hemp seeds, and baby greens. Sprinkle with flaky sea salt and crushed red pepper. Drizzle with oil.

Mole-Spiced Black Bean and Quinoa Bowl

Servings: 4

Ingredients:

- 4 cups cauliflower florets (from a 2-lb. head)
- 1 ½ teaspoons ground cumin
- 6 tablespoons olive oil, divided
- 1 ¼ teaspoons kosher salt, divided
- 1 ½ cups quinoa
- 1 15.5-oz. can black beans, drained and rinsed
- 6 tablespoons jarred red mole sauce
- 2 tablespoons red wine vinegar
- 1 tablespoon honey
- 4 cups baby arugula (about 2 oz.)
- ½ cup cotija cheese or queso fresco, crumbled (about 2 oz.)
- ¼ cup roasted pumpkin seed kernels (pepitas)
- Lime wedges, for serving (optional)

Directions:

1. Preheat oven to 450°F. Toss cauliflower, cumin, 2 tablespoons oil, and 1 teaspoon salt on a baking sheet and spread into an even layer. Roast until cauliflower is tender and caramelized, 15 to 17 minutes, stirring halfway through.
2. Meanwhile, combine 2 cups water, quinoa, and remaining ¼ teaspoon salt in a medium saucepan with a lid over high; bring to a boil. Stir and reduce heat to medium. Cover and cook until quinoa has absorbed most of the water, 12 to 14 minutes. Let stand for 5 minutes. Fluff with a fork and transfer to a large bowl; stir in beans.
3. Make dressing: Whisk mole, vinegar, honey, and remaining ¼ cup oil in a small bowl. Transfer half to quinoa mixture; add arugula and toss gently.
4. Serve cauliflower over quinoa, topped with cheese and pumpkin seeds. Drizzle with remaining dressing and serve with lime wedges, if using.

Nutrition Facts:

Calories 773   Total Fat 44g   Cholesterol 15mg   Sodium 1418mg   Total Carbohydrate 72g   Total Sugars 14g   Protein 22g

This Anti-Inflammatory Berry Matcha Smoothie Is the Best Healthy Breakfast for Busy Mornings

Servings: 1

Ingredients:

- 1 cup fresh blueberries or frozen wild blueberries
- 1/2 cup spinach
- 1/2 cup yogurt
- 1/4 cup unsweetened coconut milk, chilled
- 1 teaspoon matcha powder
- 1/2 teaspoon ground turmeric

Directions:

1. Add blueberries, 3/4 cup water, spinach, yogurt, coconut milk, matcha, and turmeric to blender and process until smooth.
2. Add ice cubes, as needed, and blend again. Serve in a tall glass, and add optional blueberries or microgreens as garnish.
3. Matcha is expensive, so store yours properly for best results. Keep matcha powder in an opaque, airtight tin in the refrigerator to preserve the antioxidants and prevent the tea from breaking down and changing color. If stored properly, it will last several months.

SEAFOOD & FISH RECIPES

Salmon & Avocado Poke Bowl

Servings: 4

Ingredients:

- Poke
- 1 pound previously frozen wild salmon, skinned and cut into 3/4-inch cubes
- 1 medium ripe avocado, diced
- ½ cup thinly sliced yellow onion
- ½ cup thinly sliced scallion greens
- ½ cup chopped fresh cilantro
- ¼ cup tobiko (flying fish roe) or other caviar
- 3 tablespoons reduced-sodium tamari
- 2 teaspoons toasted (dark) sesame oil
- ½ teaspoon Sriracha
- Brown Rice Salad
- 2 cups cooked short-grain brown rice, warmed
- 2 cups packed spicy greens, such as arugula, watercress or mizuna
- 2 tablespoons rice vinegar
- 2 tablespoons extra-virgin olive oil
- 1 tablespoon Chinese-style or Dijon mustard

Directions:

1. Gently combine salmon, avocado, onion, scallion greens, cilantro, tobiko (or caviar), tamari, sesame oil and Sriracha in a medium bowl.
2. Combine rice and greens in a large bowl. Whisk vinegar, oil and mustard in a small bowl. Add to the rice salad and mix well. Serve the poke on the rice salad.

Nutrition Facts:

Calories 442 Total Carbohydrate 34g Dietary Fiber 7g Total Sugars 4g Added Sugars 2g Protein 30g Total Fat 22g Saturated Fat 3g Cholesterol 88mg Vitamin A 3496iu Vitamin C 31mg Folate 65mcg Sodium 792mg Calcium 93mg Iron 3mg Magnesium 59mg Potassium 828mg

Sheet-Pan Shrimp & Beets

Servings: 4

Ingredients:

- 1 pound small beets, peeled and cut into 1/2-inch pieces
- 2 tablespoons extra-virgin olive oil, divided
- ¾ teaspoon salt, divided
- ¾ teaspoon ground pepper, divided

- 6 cups chopped kale
- 1 ¼ pounds extra-large raw shrimp (16-20 count), peeled and deveined
- ½ teaspoon dry mustard
- ½ teaspoon dried tarragon
- 3 tablespoons unsalted sunflower seeds, toasted

Directions:

1. Preheat oven to 425 degrees F.
2. Toss beets with 1 tablespoon oil and 1/4 teaspoon each salt and pepper in a large bowl. Spread evenly on a rimmed baking sheet. Roast for 15 minutes.
3. Toss kale with the remaining 1 tablespoon oil and 1/4 teaspoon each salt and pepper in the bowl. Stir into the beets on the baking sheet.
4. Sprinkle shrimp with mustard, tarragon and the remaining 1/4 teaspoon each salt and pepper. Place on top of the vegetables. Roast until the shrimp are cooked and the vegetables are tender, 10 to 15 minutes more.
5. Transfer the shrimp to a serving platter. Stir sunflower seeds into the vegetables and serve with the shrimp.

Nutrition Facts:

Calories 266 Total Carbohydrate 15g Dietary Fiber 5g Total Sugars 8g Protein 29g Total Fat 11g Saturated Fat 2g Cholesterol 199mg Vitamin A 2663iu Vitamin C 35mg Folate 172mcg Sodium 681mg Calcium 141mg Iron 2mg Magnesium 90mg Potassium 873mg

Salmon Farro Salad with Corn and Bacon

Cooking Time: 35 Mins.

Servings: 4

Ingredients:

- 1 cup farro
- 8 ounces salmon
- 1/2 tsp blackening seasoning
- 1 tsp avocado oil
- 4 slices bacon
- 2 ears fresh corn
- 2 cups sliced tomato
- 2 tbsp fresh chives
- Dijon Dressing
- 1 tsp dijon mustard
- 2 1/2 tbsp red wine vinegar
- 1/4 cup olive oil
- 1/4 tsp sea salt
- 1/4 tsp freshly ground black pepper

Directions:

1. Bring a large pot of salted water to boil, once boiling add 1 cup of farro and cook for 30 minutes. Drain and set aside.
2. While farro is cooking prepare bacon: Cook in a cast iron skillet until crispy. When finished set bacon aside on a dish lined with paper towels. Spill out all but 1 tsp of bacon fat from the skillet.
3. Prepare salmon by drizzling with avocado oil and coating in blackening seasoning (or salt and pepper). Sear in same skillet the bacon was cooked in. Cook for 3 minutes on each side or until cooked to medium. Flake salmon and set aside.
4. Char corn on the cob by slicing from the cob and toasting in a dry skillet.
5. Prepare dressing by whisking together all **Ingredients:**
6. Assemble: Toss farro, corn, tomatoes, and chive with dressing. Top with salmon and bacon. Serve immediately or chill in a covered container in refrigerator. Serve within 5 days.

Notes

HOW TO COOK FARRO:

Farro cooks like pasta, no need to perfectly measure the water!

There are 2 methods:

Traditional:

Bring a large pot of water to boil, add 1 cup of farro, boil for 30 minutes, drain.

Pre-soak:

Soak 1 cup of farro in water overnight or for several hours. Drain.

Bring a large pot of water to boil, add farro and boil for 10 minutes, drain.

HOW TO CHAR CORN:

Char corn over a gas stovetop. Turn on a gas burner and place corn on the cob directly over the flame. Using tongs, carefully turn the cob until you have reached peak level of char (see all that gorgeous black on the corn kernels? that is what I consider peak char level). Just be cautious because the kernels can pop and explode, making this a slightly dangerous endeavor.

OR - Remove corn from cob and char in a dry cast iron skillet. You can achieve nearly the same amount of smokey grill flavor by just toasting the kernels in a dry skillet. I prefer the open flame method, but a cast iron skillet works equally well.

OR - Use an indoor cast iron grill pan. Heat the pan until screaming hot and place your corn cobs on the grill pan. Turn carefully until charred.

Nutrition Facts:

Serving: 1serving (4 total Servings: in recipe for main course/ 6 as a side dish) | Calories: 533kcal | Carbohydrates: 51g | Protein: 21g | Fat: 28g | Saturated Fat: 6g | Cholesterol: 46mg | Sodium: 413mg | Potassium: 759mg | Fiber: 10g | Sugar: 5g | Vitamin A: 793IU | Vitamin C: 14mg | Calcium: 29mg | Iron: 2mg

Green Curry Salmon with Broccoli

Cooking Time: 15 Mins.

Servings: 4

Ingredients:

- 1 lb. wild salmon cut into 4 portions
- 2 tbsp avocado oil divided
- salt and pepper
- 4 cloves garlic chopped
- 1 large shallot chopped
- 1 tbsp fresh ginger finely chopped or grated
- 1 serrano chili sliced
- 2 tbsp green curry paste
- 1 can full fat coconut milk
- 1 tbsp fish sauce
- 4 cups broccoli florets
- cilantro, serrano chili, lime for serving

Directions:

1. Rub salmon with avocado oil (about 1/2 tsp per filet) season generously with salt and pepper.
2. Heat 1 tbsp avocado oil in a large skillet. Add salmon skin side down and sear until crispy (about 2 minutes), flip and cook for an additional 2 minutes. Remove from pan and set aside.
3. Add additional avocado oil to pan and saute garlic, shallot, ginger, and serrano chili for 3 minutes or until tender. Add curry paste and stir to coat all vegetables in curry paste. Add coconut milk and fish sauce and scrape to release any browned bits from the bottom of the pan.
4. Add broccoli florets, bring to a simmer, cover for 4 minutes or until broccoli is tender.
5. Add salmon back to the ban, spoon sauce over the salmon and simmer until salmon is warmed through.
6. Top with cilantro, lime juice, and sliced raw serrano (optional).

Notes

SERVE WITH:

Cauliflower rice

Jasmine rice

Brown rice

Zucchini noodles

Rice noodles

Nutrition Facts:

Serving: 1serving (4 total Servings: in recipe) | Calories: 463kcal | Carbohydrates: 12g | Protein: 28g | Fat: 35g | Saturated Fat: 20g | Cholesterol: 62mg | Sodium: 447mg | Potassium: 1111mg | Fiber: 3g | Sugar: 3g | Vitamin A: 1809IU | Vitamin C: 85mg | Calcium: 94mg | Iron: 5mg

Everything Crusted Tuna Meal Prep Bowls

Cooking Time: 20 Mins.

Servings: 4

Ingredients:

- 2 lbs. ahi tuna Steaks (sushi grade)
- 1/4 cup everything but the bagel seasoning *DIY instructions in **notes**
- 1 tbsp avocado oil divided
- Brussels Sprouts
- 1 lb. brussels sprouts, shredded
- 2 tbsp avocado oil
- 1/4 tsp garlic powder
- 1/4 tsp sea salt
- 1/4 tsp freshly ground black pepper
- Scallion Cauliflower Puree
- 1 lb. cauliflower florets I used a bag of frozen cauliflower
- 1 tbsp butter (or vegan alternative, olive oil works well too)
- 2 tbsp scallions, sliced (eq. one scallion)
- 1/4 tsp sea salt

Directions:

1. Tuna
2. Spead everything but the bagel seasoning on a large plate. Coat the tuna in a little avocado oil (about 1/2 tsp per tuna steak) and coat in seasoning, being sure to cover all surfaces including sides.
3. Heat a large cast iron skillet on medium-high heat for several minutes. Pour remaining avocado oil (about 2 tsp.) into skillet and sear the tuna.
4. Skillet should be quite hot so you hear a loud sizzle as the tuna hits the pan. For rare tuna cook for 2 minutes per side. I also (using tongs) gently sear all sides of the tuna to allow the seasoning to stick.
5. When cool enough to handle slice and set aside.
6. Brussels Sprouts
7. Shred brussels sprouts using a sharp knife. Alternatively, buy pre-shredded.
8. Lay shredded sprouts on a large baking sheet. Coat brussels sprouts in oil, garlic powder, salt, and pepper. Using your hands, toss well to combine.

9. Roast at 350° for 12 minutes, tossing once during cooking.
10. Cauliflower Puree
11. Place cauliflower in a small saucepan and cover with water. Bring to a boil and cook for 4-5 minutes until just tender.
12. Drain and add to blender with butter and salt.
13. Blend until creamy. Stir in scallions, or sprinkle scallions on top
14. Meal Prep Bowls
15. Fill containers with cauliflower puree, Brussels sprouts, and top with sliced tuna. Sprinkle with scallions.
16. When ready to reheat either microwave for 2 minutes or if your dish is oven-safe heat in oven until warm.
17. I cook my tuna extra rare so it can withstand a reheat.

Notes

I used a bag of organic frozen cauliflower for this recipe, but fresh works equally well.

If you can't find everything but the bagel seasoning (Trader Joe's sells it) here is a quick and easy recipe to make your own.

DIY Everything but the Bagel Seasoning:

2 tbsp sesame seeds

2 tbsp dried minced onion

2 tbsp dried minced garlic

1 tbsp poppy seeds

1 tsp sea salt flakes (maldon is my favorite, or coarse salt will also work)

Combine together and store in an air-tight jar.

Nutrition Facts:

Calories: 523kcal | Carbohydrates: 16g | Protein: 59g | Fat: 25g | Saturated Fat: 6g | Cholesterol: 93mg | Sodium: 467mg | Potassium: 1351mg | Fiber: 6g | Sugar: 4g | Vitamin A: 5925IU | Vitamin C: 151.6mg | Calcium: 91mg | Iron: 4.4mg

Easy One Pan Mediterranean Cod

Cooking Time: 30 Mins.

Servings: 4

Ingredients:

- 2 tbsp olive oil
- 1 small onion sliced
- 2 cups sliced fennel
- 3 large cloves garlic chopped
- 1 14.5 ounce can diced tomato
- 1 cup diced fresh tomatoes
- 2 cups shredded kale

- 1/2 cup water
- pinch of crushed red pepper
- 2 tsp fresh oregano or 1/2 tsp dried oregano
- 1 cup oil cured black olives
- 1 lb. cod cut into 4 portions
- 1/8 tsp salt
- 1/4 tsp black pepper
- 1/4 tsp fennel seeds optional
- 1 tsp orange zest
- garnish
- fresh oregano fennel fronds, orange zest, olive oil

Directions:

1. In a large skillet (ideally with high sides) over medium heat, cook onion, fennel, and garlic in olive oil for 8 minutes, season with salt and pepper (about 1/4 tsp of each). Add canned diced tomato, fresh tomato, kale, and water. Stir well and cook for 12 minutes. Add crushed red pepper, fresh oregano, and olives.
2. Prepare fish, season with salt, pepper, orange zest and fennel seeds (optional). Nestle fish into kale tomato stewing mixture. Cover pan and cook for 10 minutes.
3. Remove from heat, and finish with fennel fronds, more fresh oregano, more orange zest, and a drizzle of olive oil on top.
4. Serve immediately.

Notes

This is definitely a complete meal but it is also quite lovely served with a grain on the side, just be sure to pour lots of that yummy sauce over the grain

Nutrition Facts:

Calories: 257kcal | Carbohydrates: 12g | Protein: 23g | Fat: 13g | Saturated Fat: 1g | Cholesterol: 48mg | Sodium: 700mg | Potassium: 964mg | Fiber: 3g | Sugar: 2g | Vitamin A: 3895IU | Vitamin C: 55.1mg | Calcium: 129mg | Iron: 1.7mg

Mediterranean Sheet Pan Salmon with Zucchini Noodles

Cooking Time: 10 Mins.

Servings: 3

Ingredients:

- 1 lb wild salmon
- 3 cups zucchini noodles 1 large zucchini or 16 ounce of pre-spiralized zucchini
- 3/4 cup grape tomatoes
- 3/4 cup olives
- 1 small red onion, sliced sliced
- 4 cloves garlic, crushed

- 2 tbsp olive oil
- 1 tsp za'atar (see notes for substitution)
- 1/4 tsp salt
- fresh lemon wedges

Directions:

1. Preheat oven to 400°
2. Drizzle one teaspoon of olive oil on the salmon, coat with 1 clove of crushed garlic, za'atar spice (see note for substitution), and salt. Place in the center of a large baking sheet.
3. In a medium bowl toss together zucchini noodles, 3 cloves of crushed garlic, tomato, olives, onion, black pepper, and olive oil. Pour onto the baking sheet and arrange in a single layer around the salmon.
4. Roast in the oven for 10 minutes. (see notes for cooking time).
5. Remove from oven, serve immediately with fresh lemon wedges and an extra sprinkle of flaky sea salt.

Notes

Cooking Time: for Salmon:

10 minutes for medium salmon

15 minutes for medium well salmon (I don't recommend cooking beyond 15 minutes)

Za'atar Substitute:

Za'atar is a middle eastern spice blend that traditionally uses thyme, sumac, and sesame seeds. Although the one I use is from my trip to Israel and contains the ancient (biblical) spice Hyssop. You can find Za'atar blends in some specialty grocery stores, online, or make your own. Or... if all of that seems like too much trouble you can absolutely just use a pinch of dried thyme and a pinch of dried oregano, it's not the same (Za'atar purists please don't yell at me!) but it works perfectly well in this recipe.

Nutrition Facts:

Serving: 1serving | Calories: 400kcal | Carbohydrates: 11g | Protein: 33g | Fat: 24g | Saturated Fat: 3g | Cholesterol: 83mg | Sodium: 807mg | Potassium: 1476mg | Fiber: 4g | Sugar: 7g | Vitamin A: 975IU | Vitamin C: 48.7mg | Calcium: 91mg | Iron: 2.8mg

Halibut with Spiced Chickpeas and Carrots

Cooking Time: 20 Mins.

Servings: 4

Ingredients:

- 1 lb. fresh halibut filets skinned, and cut into 4 portions
- 2 tbsp olive oil
- 1 small red onion chopped (reserve 1/4 cup for pickled onion)

- 2 cloves garlic chopped
- 3 large carrots sliced
- 13.5 ounce can of chickpeas
- 1 tbsp harissa paste
- 1/4 cup chicken stock
- 1/4 tsp salt
- 1/4 tsp pepper
- Pickled Onion
- 1/4 red onion (chopped, reserved from above)
- 2 tbsp red wine vinegar
- 1/4 tsp sea salt
- 1/4 tsp sugar

Directions:

1. Preheat oven to 300°
2. In a small bowl combine 1/4 cup red onion, red wine vinegar, salt, and sugar stir well to combine and set aside.
3. In a large skillet over medium heat saute remaining onion, garlic, and carrots in olive oil for 4 minutes. Add salt and pepper, stir well to combine.
4. Add chickpeas, harissa paste, and chicken stock. Using a wooden spoon stir the harissa paste into the chicken stock. Bring to a low simmer and cook for 2-3 minutes.
5. Season the halibut well with salt and pepper, and cut into 4-6 portions. Nestle the halibut into the chickpea mixture and bake for 8-15 minutes.
6. The halibut is done when it is no longer opaque and is firm to the touch, a thinner piece will take closer to 8 minutes while a thicker piece will take closer to 15 minutes.
7. Remove from the oven and top with chopped fresh parsley and reserved pickled onion.

Spicy Crunchy Salmon and Broccoli Sheet Pan Meal

Cooking Time: 10 Mins.

Servings: 2

Ingredients:

- 2 4-6 ounce wild salmon filets
- 4 cups broccoli florets
- 2 tbsp mayonnaise
- 1 tsp sriracha sauce
- 1/2 tsp lime juice
- 2 tbsp panko breadcrumbs
- 2 tbsp extra virgin olive oil
- zest from one lime
- sea salt and black pepper
- Sesame Cucumber Salad
- 3 cups sliced cucumber about 4 small Kirby

- cucumbers
- 2 tbsp rice wine vinegar
- 2 tsp toasted sesame oil
- 1 tbsp toasted sesame seeds
- pinch crushed red pepper flakes (optional)

Directions:

1. Preheat oven to 400°
2. In a medium bowl toss together broccoli florets, olive oil, lime zest, and a generous pinch of salt and pepper. Arrange on a large baking sheet and place in oven for 5 minutes.
3. While broccoli is in the oven, combine mayonnaise, sriracha sauce, and lime juice in a small bowl and whisk to combine. Spread mayo mixture evenly over 2 salmon filets and top with panko breadcrumbs (you should need about 1 tbsp breadcrumbs for each piece of salmon)
4. After 5 minutes remove broccoli from the oven and using a spatula, create some room in the center of the sheet pan for the salmon. Gently place the salmon on the sheet pan and return to the oven for 8 minutes.
5. Remove from the oven and serve immediately. Feel free to add an extra squeeze of fresh lime juice onto each piece of salmon.
6. Sesame Cucumber Salad
7. In a medium bowl whisk together sesame oil and rice wine vinegar, toss cucumbers in dressing and top with crushed red pepper and toasted sesame seeds.

Notes

Cooking Time: for Salmon, this is for a 4-6 ounce piece of salmon. If you use a larger filet you may need to increase cooking time slighlty. Wild salmon cooks quickly and can become dry quite easily. My recommendation is to undercook slightly to retain moisture.

6 minutes for rare

8 minutes for medium-rare

10 minutes for medium

12 minutes for medium well salmon (I don't recommend cooking beyond 15 minutes)

Nutrition Facts:

Serving: 1serving | Calories: 383kcal | Carbohydrates: 20g | Protein: 8g | Fat: 32g | Saturated Fat: 5g | Cholesterol: 6mg | Sodium: 277mg | Potassium: 613mg | Fiber: 6g | Sugar: 4g | Vitamin A: 1134IU | Vitamin C: 164mg | Calcium: 143mg | Iron: 2mg

Sun-Dried Tomato Butter Salmon and Broccolini Is Your New Go-To Easy Dinner

Servings: 4

Ingredients:

- 1 lb Broccolini, trimmed, thick stalks halved lengthwise
- 1 1/2 Tbsp olive oil
- 3/4 tsp kosher salt, divided
- 3 Tbsp unsalted butter, softened
- 2 Tbsp drained and finely chopped sun-dried tomatoes
- 1/2 tsp dried Italian seasoning
- 1 clove garlic, grated on a Microplane (1/2 tsp)
- 4 6-oz skin-on salmon fillets
- 2/3 cup grated Parmesan cheese (about 1 oz.)
- Lemon wedges, for serving

Directions:

1. Preheat oven to 425°F. Toss together Broccolini, oil, and 1/2 teaspoon salt on a large-rimmed baking sheet lined with parchment paper. Bake for 7 minutes.
2. Meanwhile, stir together butter, tomatoes, Italian seasoning, garlic, and remaining 1/4 teaspoon salt in a small bowl. Spread butter mixture over flesh side of salmon.
3. Remove baking sheet from oven. Push Broccolini to outer edges; arrange salmon, skin side down, in center of baking sheet, spacing apart evenly. Roast until salmon is just opaque in center, 10 to 14 minutes.
4. Transfer salmon to plates. On baking sheet, toss Broccolini with cheese and squeeze a lemon wedge over top. Serve with salmon and more lemon wedges.

Nutrition Facts:

Calories 582 Total Fat 40g Saturated Fat 13g Cholesterol 144mg Sodium 678mg Total Carbohydrate 10g Dietary Fiber 4g Total Sugars 2g Protein 45g Vitamin C 66mg Calcium 246mg Iron 2mg Potassium 1067mg

Salmon Tacos With Grapefruit Salsa

Servings: 6

Ingredients:

- 4 salmon fillets
- 3/4 tsp ground cumin
- 3/4 tsp smoked paprika
- 1 1/4 tsp kosher salt
- 1/2 tsp crushed red pepper
- 2 tbsp olive oil
- 1 avocado, chopped
- 1 large grapefruit, peeled, sliced into sections over a bowl, and chopped into 1/2-in. pieces, juice reserved
- 1/2 cup fresh cilantro
- 3 medium scallions
- 1 jalapeno, finely chopped
- 12 corn tortillas, warmed
- 1 tbsp sour cream

Directions:

1. Pat salmon dry. Stir together cumin, paprika, 3/4 teaspoon salt, and crushed red pepper in a small bowl. Sprinkle mixture on flesh sides of fillets.
2. Heat a large cast-iron skillet over medium-high; add oil. When oil is hot, carefully place salmon in skillet, skin side down. Reduce heat to medium and gently press each fillet with a spatula to flatten. Cook until salmon is opaque 3/4 of the way up sides, 6 to 7 minutes. Flip and cook until just cooked through, 1 to 2 minutes.
3. Stir together avocado, grapefruit, grapefruit juice, cilantro, scallions, jalapeño, and remaining 1/2 teaspoon salt in a medium bowl.
4. Break salmon into large pieces and serve on tortillas with grapefruit salsa and, if using, sour cream.

Smoky Sheet Pan Salmon and Potatoes

Servings: 4

Ingredients:

- 2 navel oranges
- 3 tablespoons olive oil
- 1 tablespoon smoked paprika
- 2 teaspoons dried oregano
- 24 ounce baby Yukon Gold potatoes, halved
- 1 ½ teaspoons kosher salt, divided
- 4 6-oz. skin-on salmon fillets, patted dry
- 2 avocados, chopped
- ½ cup loosely packed fresh cilantro leaves
- ¼ cup fresh lime juice (from 4 limes)

Directions:

1. Preheat oven to 425°F. Zest 1 orange to yield 1 teaspoon and place zest in a small bowl. Remove rind from oranges and cut flesh into segments. Place segments in a medium bowl. Add oil, paprika, and oregano to orange zest; stir to combine.

2. Toss potatoes with 2 tablespoons oil mixture and ¾ teaspoon salt on a parchment-lined large rimmed baking sheet. Bake until golden and mostly tender, about 25 minutes.

3. Sprinkle salmon with ½ teaspoon salt and rub with remaining 1½ tablespoons oil mixture. Place salmon, skin side down, on baking sheet with potatoes. Bake until salmon is cooked to desired degree of doneness, 12 to 15 minutes for medium.

4. Meanwhile, add avocados, cilantro, lime juice, and remaining ¼ teaspoon salt to orange segments; stir to combine. Serve over salmon and potatoes.

Nutrition Facts:

Per Serving: 660 Calories; Fat 35g; Cholesterol 90mg; Sodium 865mg; Carbohydrates 51g; Dietary Fiber 12g; Protein 42g; Sugars 9g; Saturated Fat 6g.

Soy-Glazed Salmon Sandwiches With Watercress

Servings: 4

Ingredients:

- ¼ cup sweet chili sauce
- 2 tablespoons soy sauce
- 1 tablespoon unseasoned rice vinegar
- 2 tablespoons canola oil, divided
- 4 5-oz. skinless salmon fillets
- ½ teaspoon kosher salt
- ½ teaspoon freshly ground black pepper
- 2 cups watercress, tough stems removed
- 5 radishes, thinly sliced
- 1 tablespoon fresh lemon juice (from 1 lemon)
- ¼ cup mayonnaise
- 4 brioche hamburger buns, split and toasted
- Sweet potato chips, for serving

Directions:

1. Mix chili sauce, soy sauce, and vinegar in a bowl.

2. Heat 1 tablespoon oil in a heavy pan over medium-high. Season salmon with salt and pepper. Cook until browned on 1 side, about 3 minutes. Flip and cook, brushing with soy mixture often, until just cooked through, about 3 minutes.

3. Toss watercress, radishes, lemon juice, and remaining 1 tablespoon oil in a medium bowl.
4. Spread mayonnaise on top and bottom halves of buns. Build sandwiches with salmon and watercress mixture. Serve sandwiches with sweet potato chips.

Nutrition Facts:

Calories 632   Cholesterol 125mg   Sodium 1333mg   Total Carbohydrate 45g   Total Sugars 5g   Protein 37g

Sheet Pan Salmon With Potatoes and Broccolini

Servings: 4

Ingredients:

- 1 pound small Yukon Gold potatoes, halved
- ½ cup olive oil, divided
- 1 ¼ teaspoon kosher salt, divided
- ¾ teaspoon black pepper, divided
- 4 6-oz. salmon fillets
- 1 pound Broccolini, trimmed
- 2 tablespoons fresh lemon juice (from 1 lemon)
- 1 shallot, finely chopped
- 1 ½ teaspoon Dijon mustard

Directions:

1. Preheat oven to 450°F. Toss potatoes with 2 tablespoons oil, ½ teaspoon salt, and ¼ teaspoon pepper on a rimmed baking sheet. Roast for 15 minutes.
2. Meanwhile, rub salmon with 1 tablespoon oil and season with ½ teaspoon each salt and pepper. Add salmon to sheet and roast until potatoes are tender, 5 more minutes.
3. Turn potatoes, add Broccolini to sheet, and drizzle with 1 tablespoon oil. Heat broiler and broil all until salmon and Broccolini are browned, 2 to 3 minutes.
4. Whisk lemon juice, shallot, and mustard with remaining ¼ cup oil and ¼ teaspoon salt and drizzle over salmon and vegetables.

SIDE DISHES, SNACKS & VEGETARIAN RECIPES

Roasted Vegetable & Black Bean Tacos

Servings: 2

Ingredients:

- 1 cup roasted root vegetables (see associated recipe)
- ½ cup cooked or canned black beans, rinsed
- 2 teaspoons extra-virgin olive oil
- 1 teaspoon ground cumin
- 1 teaspoon chili powder
- ½ teaspoon ground coriander
- ¼ teaspoon kosher salt
- ¼ teaspoon ground pepper
- 4 corn tortillas, lightly toasted or warmed
- ½ avocado, cut into 8 slices
- 1 lime, cut into wedges
- Chopped fresh cilantro & salsa for garnish

Directions:

1. Combine roasted root vegetables, beans, oil, cumin, chili powder, coriander, salt and pepper in a saucepan. Cover and cook over medium-low heat until heated through, 6 to 8 minutes.
2. Divide the mixture among the tortillas. Top with avocado. Serve with lime wedges. Garnish with cilantro and/or salsa, if desired.

Nutrition Facts:

Calories 343   Total Carbohydrate 44g   Dietary Fiber 12g   Total Sugars 6g   Protein 8g   Total Fat 17g   Saturated Fat 2g   Vitamin A 3365iu   Vitamin C 13mg   Folate 101mcg   Sodium 352mg   Calcium 97mg   Iron 3mg   Magnesium 64mg   Potassium 701mg

Quinoa Chili with Sweet Potatoes

Servings: 5

Ingredients:

- 1 tablespoon extra-virgin olive oil
- 2 (12 ounce) sweet potatoes, peeled and cut into 1/2-inch pieces
- 1 medium yellow onion, diced
- 2 poblano peppers, diced
- 4 large cloves garlic, chopped
- 1 tablespoon chili powder

- 2 teaspoons ground cumin
- 4 cups unsalted vegetable broth
- 1 (10 ounce) can no-salt-added diced tomatoes with green chiles
- 1 (4 ounce) can diced green chiles
- 2 cups water, divided
- 1 cup uncooked white or multicolored quinoa
- 1 (15 ounce) can no-salt-added pinto beans, rinsed
- ½ teaspoon salt
- Sliced jalapeño peppers, yogurt and cilantro for serving

Directions:

1. Heat oil in a large pot over medium-high heat. Add sweet potatoes and cook, stirring occasionally, until slightly softened and lightly charred, 6 to 7 minutes. Add onion and poblanos; cook, stirring occasionally, until slightly softened, about 3 minutes. Add garlic, chili powder and cumin; cook, stirring constantly, until fragrant, about 30 seconds. Add broth, tomatoes, green chiles and 1 cup water. Cover, increase heat to high and bring to a boil.
2. Stir in quinoa, beans and salt. Reduce heat to medium, cover and simmer, stirring occasionally, until the quinoa is tender, about 15 minutes, adding the remaining 1 cup water during the last 3 minutes of cook time. Garnish with jalapeño slices, yogurt and cilantro, if desired.
3. To make ahead
4. Refrigerate chili in an airtight container for up to 5 days or freeze for up to 2 months.

Nutrition Facts:

Calories 346 Total Carbohydrate 63g   Dietary Fiber 11g   Total Sugars 11g   Protein 12g   Total Fat 6g   Saturated Fat 1g   Vitamin A 10763iu   Sodium 703mg   Potassium 862mg

One-Pot Lemon-Broccoli Pasta with Parmesan

Servings: 4

Ingredients:

- 2 tablespoons extra-virgin olive oil
- 1 medium shallot, minced
- 2 cloves garlic, minced
- 8 ounces whole-wheat rotini or farfalle pasta
- 1 ¾ cups water
- 1 ½ cups low-sodium vegetable broth or chicken broth
- 1 tablespoon lemon zest
- ½ teaspoon salt
- ½ teaspoon ground pepper

- 1 (10 ounce) package frozen broccoli florets, thawed and coarsely chopped
- 1/3 cup grated Parmesan cheese
- 4 teaspoons lemon juice, or more to taste

Directions:

1. Heat oil in a large saucepan over medium heat. Add shallot and cook, stirring, until starting to soften, about 2 minutes. Add garlic and cook, stirring, until fragrant, about 30 seconds. Add pasta, water, broth, lemon zest, salt and pepper. Cover and bring to a boil. Uncover, reduce heat to medium-high and cook, stirring frequently, for 10 minutes. Add broccoli and cook, stirring, until heated through, 2 to 3 minutes. Remove from heat and stir in Parmesan and lemon juice.

Nutrition Facts:

Calories 210 Total Carbohydrate 24g   Dietary Fiber 5g Total Sugars 2g   Protein 9g   Total Fat 10g   Saturated Fat 2g   Cholesterol 6mg   Vitamin A 744iu   Vitamin C 31mg   Folate 51mcg   Sodium 451mg   Calcium 100mg Iron 2mg   Magnesium 45mg   Potassium 257mg

Buffalo Cauliflower Tacos

Servings: 6

Ingredients:

- 6 cups cauliflower florets
- ½ cup Buffalo-style hot sauce
- 2 tablespoons extra-virgin olive oil, plus 1 1/2 teaspoons, divided
- 1/3 cup shredded Cheddar cheese
- 1 ½ cups fresh corn kernels
- 1 ½ cups finely shredded romaine lettuce
- 1 medium avocado, sliced
- 12 (6-inch) corn tortillas, warmed
- ½ cup ranch dressing

Directions:

2. Place rack in upper third of oven; preheat to 425°F. Line a large rimmed baking sheet with parchment paper. Combine cauliflower, Buffalo sauce and 2 tablespoons oil in a large bowl; toss well to coat. Spread in an even layer on the prepared baking sheet. Roast until the cauliflower starts to brown and is almost tender, 12 to 14 minutes. Remove from oven and sprinkle evenly with cheese. Continue roasting until the cauliflower is tender, 8 to 10 minutes. Set aside until ready to serve.
3. Heat a large nonstick skillet over medium-high heat.

Add corn and the remaining 1 1/2 teaspoons oil; cook, stirring occasionally, until the corn is blistered and charred, about 5 minutes. Remove from heat.

4. Divide the cauliflower, lettuce, corn and avocado evenly among warm tortillas. Drizzle evenly with ranch dressing. Serve immediately.

Nutrition Facts:

Calories 374   Total Carbohydrate 43g   Dietary Fiber 8g   Total Sugars 3g   Protein 9g   Total Fat 21g   Saturated Fat 4g   Cholesterol 11mg   Vitamin A 1417iu   Sodium 877mg

Roasted Root Veggies & Greens over Spiced Lentils

Servings: 2

Ingredients:

- Lentils
- 1 ½ cups water
- ½ cup black beluga lentils or French green lentils (see Tip)
- 1 teaspoon garlic powder
- ½ teaspoon ground coriander
- ½ teaspoon ground cumin
- ¼ teaspoon ground allspice
- ¼ teaspoon kosher salt
- ⅛ teaspoon sumac (optional)
- 2 tablespoons lemon juice
- 1 teaspoon extra-virgin olive oil
- Vegetables
- 1 tablespoon extra-virgin olive oil
- 1 clove garlic, smashed
- 1 1/2 cups roasted root vegetables (see associated recipes)
- 2 cups chopped kale or beet greens
- 1 teaspoon ground coriander
- ⅛ teaspoon ground pepper
- Pinch of kosher salt
- 2 tablespoons tahini or low-fat plain yogurt
- Fresh parsley for garnish

Directions:

1. To prepare lentils: Combine water, lentils, garlic powder, 1/2 teaspoon coriander, cumin, allspice, 1/4 teaspoon salt and sumac (if using) in a medium pot. Bring to a boil. Reduce heat to maintain a simmer, cover and cook until tender, 25 to 30 minutes.

2. Uncover and continue simmering until the liquid reduces slightly, about 5 minutes more. Drain. Stir in lemon juice and 1 teaspoon oil.

3. Meanwhile, to prepare vegetables: Heat oil in a large skillet over medium heat. Add garlic and cook until fragrant, 1 to 2 minutes. Add roasted root vegetables and cook, stirring often, until heated through, 2 to 4 minutes. Stir in kale (or beet greens) and cook until just wilted, 2 to 3 minutes. Stir in coriander, pepper and salt.
4. Serve the vegetables over the lentils, topped with tahini (or yogurt). Garnish with parsley, if desired.

Tip

We like black beluga lentils or French green lentils instead of brown when we want lentils that hold their shape (instead of breaking down) when cooked. Look for them in natural-foods stores and some supermarkets.

Nutrition Facts:

Calories 453 Total Carbohydrate 50g   Dietary Fiber 14g   Total Sugars 5g   Protein 18g   Total Fat 22g   Saturated Fat 3g   Vitamin A 5939iu   Vitamin C 35mg   Folate 81mcg   Sodium 346mg   Calcium 114mg   Iron 5mg   Magnesium 45mg   Potassium 465mg

Baked Eggs in Tomato Sauce with Kale

Servings: 4

Ingredients:

- 1 tablespoon extra-virgin olive oil
- 3 10-ounce packages frozen chopped kale, thawed, drained and squeezed dry (9 cups)
- ½ teaspoon salt, divided
- ¼ teaspoon ground pepper, divided
- 1 25-ounce jar low-sodium marinara sauce or 3 cups canned low-sodium tomato sauce
- 8 large eggs

Directions:

1. Preheat oven to 350 degrees F.
2. Heat oil in a 10-inch cast-iron skillet or nonstick ovenproof skillet over medium heat. Add kale, season with 1/4 teaspoon salt and 1/8 teaspoon pepper, and sauté for 2 minutes. Stir in marinara (or tomato) sauce and bring to a simmer.
3. Make 8 wells in the sauce with the back of a spoon and carefully crack an egg into each well. Season the eggs with the remaining 1/4 teaspoon salt and 1/8 teaspoon pepper.
4. Transfer the pan to the oven and bake until the egg

whites are set and the yolks are still soft, about 20 minutes.

Nutrition Facts:

Calories 344 Total Carbohydrate 21g Dietary Fiber 6g Total Sugars 7g Protein 21g Total Fat 20g Saturated Fat 4g Cholesterol 372mg Vitamin A 15012iu Vitamin C 91mg Folate 83mcg Sodium 653mg Calcium 377mg Iron 5mg Magnesium 51mg Potassium 848mg

Black Bean-Quinoa Bowl

Servings: 1

Ingredients:

- ¾ cup canned black beans, rinsed
- 2/3 cup cooked quinoa
- ¼ cup hummus
- 1 tablespoon lime juice
- ¼ medium avocado, diced
- 3 tablespoons pico de gallo
- 2 tablespoons chopped fresh cilantro

Directions:

1. Combine beans and quinoa in a bowl. Stir hummus and lime juice together in a small bowl; thin with water to desired consistency. Drizzle the hummus dressing over the beans and quinoa. Top with avocado, pico de gallo and cilantro.

Tips

To make ahead: Assemble Buddha bowl up to 1 day in advance, with dressing on the side. To prevent avocado from browning if making ahead, toss with a squeeze of lime juice after dicing.

Nutrition Facts:

Calories 500 Total Carbohydrate 74g Dietary Fiber 20g Total Sugars 11g Protein 20g Total Fat 16g Saturated Fat 2g Vitamin A 391iu Vitamin C 16mg Folate 238mcg Sodium 612mg Calcium 114mg Iron 7mg Magnesium 139mg Potassium 1086mg

Chickpea & Quinoa Bowl with Roasted Red Pepper Sauce

Servings: 4

Ingredients:

- 1 (7 ounce) jar roasted red peppers, rinsed
- ¼ cup slivered almonds
- 4 tablespoons extra-virgin olive oil, divided
- 1 small clove garlic, minced
- 1 teaspoon paprika
- ½ teaspoon ground cumin
- ¼ teaspoon crushed red pepper (optional)
- 2 cups cooked quinoa

- ¼ cup Kalamata olives, chopped
- ¼ cup finely chopped red onion
- 1 (15 ounce) can chickpeas, rinsed
- 1 cup diced cucumber
- ¼ cup crumbled feta cheese
- 2 tablespoons finely chopped fresh parsley

Directions:

2. Place peppers, almonds, 2 tablespoons oil, garlic, paprika, cumin and crushed red pepper (if using) in a mini food processor. Puree until fairly smooth.
3. Combine quinoa, olives, red onion and the remaining 2 tablespoons oil in a medium bowl.
4. To serve, divide the quinoa mixture among 4 bowls and top with equal amounts of the chickpeas, cucumber and the red pepper sauce. Sprinkle with feta and parsley.
5. To make ahead
6. Prepare red pepper sauce (Step 1) and quinoa (Step 2); refrigerate in separate containers. Assemble just before serving.

Nutrition Facts:

Calories 479 Total Carbohydrate 50g   Dietary Fiber 8g Total Sugars 3g   Protein 13g   Total Fat 25g Saturated Fat 4g   Cholesterol 8mg   Vitamin A 1146iu Vitamin C 10mg   Folate 106mcg   Sodium 646mg Calcium 136mg   Iron 4mg   Magnesium 110mg Potassium 443mg

Korean Seasoned Kale and Spinach

Cooking Time: 2 Mins.

Servings: 6

Ingredients:

- 1 large head of kale stripped from stem and leaves chopped
- 32 ounces baby spinach
- 3 tbsp soy sauce
- 1 tbsp sesame oil
- 1 tbsp rice vinegar
- 2 tsp coconut palm sugar
- 1 tbsp Korean chili pepper flakes, Gochugaru
- 2 large garlic cloves crushed
- 3 scallions chopped, white and green part
- 1 tbsp sesame seeds

Directions:

1. Prepare kale by ripping from stems and chopping into bite size pieces.
2. Put a large pot of water on to boil, salt generously.
3. Once boiling drop kale leaves in and allow to cook for 2-3 minutes until they are bright green. Remove from pot and gently squeeze to remove some of the

moisture (I do this by pressing a wooden spoon into the spoon I am using to remove the greens).

4. Repeat with spinach.
5. In a medium bowl whisk together remaining ingredients.
6. Toss greens with dressing, top with sesame seeds.
7. Serve immediately or store in the refrigerator for 7 days. Wonderful warm, hot or chilled.

Notes

RECIPE TIPS:

I blanch the kale and spinach for this recipe - it will produce a tender green and reduce the cooking time down to approximately 2 minutes.

I do not find it necessary to shock the greens in cold water after blanching. I just remove from the salted boiling water after 2 minutes.

I use a kitchen spider to remove the greens or you could use a large slotted spoon. Once removed from the boiling water gently press down on the greens with another spoon to squeeze out some liquid.

Add to a bowl and toss with your dressing!

WHAT IS BLANCHING?

Blanching is a technique where you briefly immerse food (i.e. greens) in boiling water, typically this is followed by "shocking" the food in an ice-water bath.

Blanching will soften vegetables and intensify the color.

Nutrition Facts:

Calories: 81kcal | Carbohydrates: 9g | Protein: 6g | Fat: 4g | Saturated Fat: 1g | Sodium: 630mg | Potassium: 932mg | Fiber: 4g | Sugar: 2g | Vitamin A: 15187IU | Vitamin C: 55mg | Calcium: 185mg | Iron: 5mg

Beet Sumac Hummus

Servings: 6

Ingredients:

- 1 13.5 ouncecan of chickpeas, drained
- 1 cup roasted beets
- see note for how to roast your own or use a packaged roasted beet*
- 1/4 cup tahini
- 2 tbsp fresh lemon juice
- 1 tsp sea salt
- 2 tsp dried sumac

Directions:

1. Combine all ingredients in a food processor, process until smooth. If too thick add a bit of olive oil, or the liquid from the chickpea can.
2. Serve with veggies or pita chips. Sprinkle additional sumac on top and a drizzle of olive oil.

Notes

How to Roast Beets:

Preheat oven to 400°

Prepare a baking sheet with parchment paper

Scrub beets well and place on parchment paper (you can also wrap in parchment paper)

Roast for 40-60 minutes, checking every 20 minutes. If the beets are looking to dry add a drizzle of water. The size of the beet will determine how long they need to cook.

You know beets are done when you can easily skewer through the center (with a fork or skewer stick)

Allow beets to cool. When cool enough to touch peel with a peeler or by rubbing the skin off with a dish towel.

Nutrition Facts:

Serving: 1serving | Calories: 70kcal | Carbohydrates: 5g | Protein: 2g | Fat: 5g | Saturated Fat: 1g | Sodium: 409mg | Potassium: 120mg | Fiber: 1g | Sugar: 2g | Vitamin C: 3mg | Calcium: 18mg | Iron: 1mg

Thai Red Vegetable Curry

Cooking Time: 25 Mins.

Servings: 4

Ingredients:

- 1 tbsp coconut oil
- 1 medium red bell pepper sliced
- 1 medium onion sliced in half moons
- 4 cloves garlic sliced
- 1 tbsp fresh ginger, grated
- 1 tbsp thai red curry paste
- 1 (13.5 ounce) can coconut milk
- 1 cup vegetable stock
- 1 tbsp fish sauce
- 1 tsp coconut palm sugar
- 1 head cauliflower about 2-3 cups of florets
- 4 cups baby spinach about 5 ounces
- 2 tbsp lime juice (juice for one lime)
- fresh cilantro
- lime wedges

Directions:

1. Warm coconut oil in a large pot over medium-high heat. Add sliced bell peppers, onions, and garlic. Saute for 5 minutes.

2. Add ginger and curry paste, stir well to incorporate. Slowly stir in coconut milk, vegetable broth, fish

sauce, and coconut palm sugar. Bring to a slow boil. Add cauliflower florets, reduce heat to a low simmer, cover and cook until cauliflower is tender about 15-20 minutes. Check at the 10-minute mark and give a gentle stir.

3. Add spinach, cover and allow to wilt (2-3 minutes). Stir well. Add lime juice, stir well.
4. Serve piping hot with fresh cilantro and additional lime wedges. Serve with rice, quinoa, or noodles if preferred.

Notes

Variations on THE BEST Thai Red Vegetable Curry:

Add 1 pound of shrimp (peeled and deveined) - add to pot before you add the spinach, cook for 2 minutes or until the shrimp is no longer opaque, continue with the rest of the recipe as written.

Add shredded chicken. If you have leftover chicken and want to add more protein to the dish simply shred the chicken and add to the pot before you add the spinach. Replace the cauliflower with broccoli, cauliflower is still my favorite in this recipe but broccoli works equally well. Replace spinach with any other leafy green. I've made the recipe with kale, swiss chard, collard greens, and mustard greens. They all work well. Depending on the toughness of the green you will need to cook longer. Spinach wilts in about 2-4 minutes, collard greens will take considerably longer.

Nutrition Facts:

Serving: 1bowl | Calories: 112kcal | Carbohydrates: 16g | Protein: 4g | Fat: 4g | Saturated Fat: 3g | Sodium: 660mg | Potassium: 725mg | Fiber: 4g | Sugar: 7g | Vitamin A: 4460IU | Vitamin C: 121.3mg | Calcium: 78mg | Iron: 1.7mg

Creamy Pumpkin Cauliflower Curry with Chickpeas

Cooking Time: 20 Mins.

Servings: 4

Ingredients:

- 1 tbsp coconut oil
- 1 cup sliced onion
- 4 cloves garlic chopped
- 1 tbsp chopped ginger
- 3 cups cauliflower florets
- 1 can chickpeas rinsed
- 1 cup vegetable stock
- 1 cup coconut milk
- 3/4 cup pumpkin purée
- 1.5 tbsp curry powder
- 1/2 tsp salt

- 1 tsp turmeric
- pinch black pepper
- Juice from 1/2 a lime
- Fresh cilantro and extra lime for serving

Directions:

1. In a medium pot over medium heat melt coconut oil. Add onions, garlic, and ginger and cook for 5 minutes until onions are tender.
2. Add cauliflower, chickpeas, and vegetable stock. Simmer partially covered for 5 minutes.
3. Remove cover add coconut milk, pumpkin, curry powder, salt, turmeric, and black pepper. Stir well to combine. Cook for 10 minutes, stirring every few minutes.
4. Remove from heat, stir in lime juice.
5. Serve over rice with fresh cilantro and lime wedges.

Nutrition Facts:

Calories: 209kcal | Carbohydrates: 16g | Protein: 4g | Fat: 16g | Saturated Fat: 13g | Sodium: 562mg | Potassium: 563mg | Fiber: 4g | Sugar: 5g | Vitamin A: 7300IU | Vitamin C: 42.8mg | Calcium: 65mg | Iron: 3.9mg

Creamy Kale and Mushroom Stuffed Delicata Squash

Cooking Time: 30 Mins.

Servings: 4

Ingredients:

- 2 delicata squash
- 2 tbsp coconut oil, melted
- salt and pepper
- Fresh herbs, bay leaf, thyme, rosemary
- 1 shallot
- 16 ounces cremini mushrooms
- 1 large head kale about 6 cups
- 1/2 cup coconut cream or full fat coconut milk
- 2 tbsp coconut oil
- 1/4 tsp salt
- 1/8 tsp black pepper

Directions:

1. Preheat oven to 400°
2. Prepare the delicata squash by washing the skin, slicing in half lengthwise, and scooping out the seeds. Rub with 2 tbsp melted coconut oil, salt, and pepper.
3. Scatter fresh herbs around the delicata squash. You can use a mixture of bay leaf, sage, thyme, and

rosemary, or really any herbs that you like. Flip the squash flesh side down on a baking sheet trapping fresh herbs underneath. Roast in the oven for 20 - 30 minutes or until a knife can easily pierce through the skin. Remove from the oven and set aside.

4. While the squash is cooking prepare the kale and mushrooms: In a large skillet over medium heat, melt the coconut oil, saute shallot for 2-3 minutes until tender. Add mushrooms and saute for 4 minutes, season with salt and pepper. Add kale and stir well to wilt (about 3-4 minutes). Add coconut cream (or coconut milk) and stir well to coat all veggies.

5. Arrange squash on a platter, discarding the cooked fresh herbs (you can use new fresh herbs as a garnish on the platter) fill the cavity of each squash with the kale and mushroom mixture. Serve immediately.

Nutrition Facts:

Calories: 282kcal | Carbohydrates: 30g | Protein: 8g | Fat: 18g | Saturated Fat: 15g | Sodium: 176mg | Potassium: 1579mg | Fiber: 5g | Sugar: 7g | Vitamin A: 6343IU | Vitamin C: 68mg | Calcium: 136mg | Iron: 3mg

This Tofu Fried Rice Recipe Is a Weeknight Dinner Must

Servings: 4

Ingredients:

- 1 14-oz. pkg. firm tofu, drained
- 1/4 cup plus 2 Tbsp olive oil, divided
- 2 Tbsp. thinly sliced garlic (from 4 large cloves)
- 1 Tbsp finely chopped fresh ginger
- 1 Tbsp ground turmeric
- 1/2 cup raisins, divided
- 3 cups leftover cooked long-grain white rice (such as basmati), any clumps broken up
- 1 cup chopped fresh cilantro
- 1 Tbsp fresh lemon juice (from 1 lemon)
- 1 1/2 tsp kosher salt
- Plain whole-milk dairy or nondairy yogurt, for topping (optional)

Directions:

1. Wrap tofu in a clean kitchen towel. Press to remove excess moisture. (It's OK if tofu falls apart.) Place tofu in a medium bowl and crumble into small pieces.

2. Heat 1/4 cup oil in a large nonstick skillet over medium. Add garlic, ginger, turmeric, and 1/4 cup

raisins; cook, stirring often, until garlic is softened, about 2 minutes. Add crumbled tofu; cook, stirring constantly, until tofu absorbs turmeric oil, about 30 seconds.

3. Add rice and remaining 2 tablespoons oil to skillet; stir until thoroughly combined. Spread rice in an even layer and cook, undisturbed, until rice and tofu are crisp in spots, about 3 minutes. Stir and gently press rice into an even layer again. Cook, undisturbed, until rice and tofu are crisp in spots, about 3 minutes. Remove from heat. Stir in cilantro, lemon juice, salt, and remaining 1/4 cup raisins. Serve drizzled with yogurt, if desired.

Summer Squash Farro Bowl

Servings: 4

Ingredients:

- 1 15-oz. can low-sodium chickpeas, drained and rinsed
- 2 medium zucchini, sliced into 1-in.-thick half-moons (about 2 cups)
- 2 medium yellow squash, sliced into 1-in.-thick half-moons (about 2 cups)
- 1 red onion, sliced (1 cup)
- ¼ cup olive oil, divided
- 1 ¾ teaspoons kosher salt, divided
- 1 ¼ cups farro
- 1 teaspoon lime zest plus ¼ cup fresh juice, divided (from 2 limes)
- 1 avocado, sliced
- Fresh cilantro leaves, for serving
- ¾ cup plain whole-milk Greek yogurt

Directions:

1. Preheat oven to 450°F. Line a baking sheet with parchment paper. Toss chickpeas, zucchini, squash, onion, 2 tablespoons oil, and 1 teaspoon salt on baking sheet. Roast until zucchini and squash are browned and chickpeas are crisp, 20 to 25 minutes.

2. Meanwhile, prepare farro according to package directions. Drain; transfer to a large bowl. Stir in 2 tablespoons lime juice and remaining 2 tablespoons oil and ¾ teaspoon salt.

3. Divide farro mixture among bowls and top with squash mixture, sliced avocado, and cilantro. Stir yogurt, lime zest, and remaining 2 tablespoons lime juice in a small bowl. Serve with farro bowls for dolloping.

Nutrition Facts:

Calories 671 Total Fat 27g Cholesterol 6mg Sodium 900mg Total Carbohydrate 85g Total Sugars 11g

Protein 24g

Tofu and Mushroom Larb

Servings: 4

Ingredients:

- 1 14-oz. package extra-firm tofu, drained
- ¼ cup melted unrefined coconut oil, divided
- 8 oz. sliced shiitake mushrooms (about 4 cups), divided
- ¼ teaspoon kosher salt
- 3 ½ tablespoons fresh lime juice (from 2 limes), plus wedges for serving
- 2 tablespoons fish sauce or tamari
- 2 ½ teaspoons packed light brown sugar
- ½ teaspoon crushed red pepper
- 1 shallot, very thinly sliced
- 3 scallions, white and light green parts finely chopped (¼ cup)
- ½ cup chopped fresh cilantro leaves (from 1 bunch), divided
- ½ cup chopped roasted, salted cashews
- ½ cup lightly packed fresh mint leaves, torn if large
- 1 small head red cabbage, quartered and leaves separated
- Cooked sushi rice, for serving

Directions:

1. Press tofu between paper towels to absorb liquid. Crumble into a bowl, leaving some large pieces.
2. Heat 1 tablespoon oil in a large nonstick skillet over medium-high. Add half of mushrooms and cook, undisturbed, until golden, about 3 minutes. Toss; cook until browned, about 2 minutes. Transfer to a plate. Repeat with 1 tablespoon oil and remaining mushrooms. Season with salt.
3. Heat remaining 2 tablespoons oil over medium-high. Add tofu; cook, undisturbed, until golden brown on underside, about 5 minutes. Toss; cook until golden and crispy, 4 to 5 minutes. Remove from heat. Stir in mushrooms, lime juice, fish sauce, sugar, and crushed red pepper. Add shallot, scallions, and half of cilantro; toss. Top with cashews, mint, and remaining cilantro. Scoop onto cabbage leaves; serve with rice and lime wedges.
4. Tofu
5. This go-to plant protein, made from soybeans, is a nutritional powerhouse, since it boasts all nine essential amino acids. It also has a range of vitamins and minerals, including bone-building calcium and energy-boosting iron.

Whole Roasted Cauliflower With Grapes and Feta

Servings: 4

Ingredients:

- 1 medium head cauliflower (about 2½ pounds)
- 1 shallot, finely chopped (about 1/3 cup)
- 2 tablespoons red wine vinegar
- .25 cup olive oil, divided
- ¾ teaspoon kosher salt, divided, plus more for water
- 1 (1-pound.) block feta cheese, drained and patted dry
- 1 pound seedless red or black grapes (3 cups)
- fresh oregano leaves, roughly chopped, for serving

Directions:

1. Bring a large, tall pot of generously salted water to a boil over high. Trim cauliflower stem so head can stand upright on its own. Gently lower cauliflower into pot, standing upright. Cook, stirring occasionally, until soft when gently pierced with a fork, 10 to 12 minutes.
2. Meanwhile, preheat oven to 500 F with rack in upper third. Stir shallot and vinegar in a small bowl.
3. Gently remove cauliflower from water with a large-handled strainer, a spider, or 2 slotted spoons; transfer to a plate. Pat with paper towels to absorb any excess water. Let cool for 10 minutes. Pat dry again, then transfer to a baking sheet.
4. Brush cauliflower all over with 1 tablespoon oil and season with ½ teaspoon salt. Roast until browned in parts, about 15 minutes. Meanwhile, cut feta into 12 (½-inch thick) slices.
5. Add grapes to baking sheet with cauliflower. Drizzle with 1 tablespoon oil. Return to oven and roast for 10 minutes. Brush feta on both sides with 1 tablespoon oil; add to baking sheet. Return to oven and roast until feta forms a golden crust, cauliflower is golden brown all over, and grapes have softened, 10 to 12 minutes.
6. Brush cauliflower all over with remaining 1 tablespoon oil and season with remaining ¼ teaspoon salt. Transfer cauliflower, grapes, and feta to a platter. Drizzle with shallot mixture. Top with oregano.
7. Make It Vegan:
8. No feta, no problem. Cook plant-based sausage right on the baking sheet. Voilà—a complete meal.

SOUPS, STEW & SALADS RECIPES

Slow Cooker Sweet Potato, Apple, & Turmeric Soup

Servings: 6

Ingredients:

- 1 medium yellow onion cut into 2-inch pieces
- 3 garlic cloves peeled and smashed
- 2 pounds sweet potatoes scrubbed and cut into 2-inch pieces
- ½ pound russet potatoes scrubbed and cut into 2-inch pieces
- 1 pound apples* cored and cut into 2-inch pieces
- 1-3 teaspoons kosher salt to taste
- 1 teaspoon turmeric
- 32- oz vegetable stock can substitute chicken stock
- 1 tablespoon apple cider vinegar
- 1 cup coconut milk from a can
- Freshly ground black pepper for serving

Directions:

1. Place the onion, garlic, sweet potatoes, russet potatoes, apples, salt, turmeric and stock in the base of a 6-quart slow cooker, stirring to combine. Cover and cook on high for 3-4 hours or low for 5-6, or until the vegetables are very tender.
2. Uncover and add the apple cider vinegar and coconut milk. Using an immersion blender, blend until very smooth. Alternatively, working in batches, carefully ladle the soup into a blender and blend on high until smooth. Taste and add additional salt or vinegar if you like.

Notes

Serving Suggestions: Top with Smokey Maple Roasted Chickpeas and/or cooked chicken sausage, freshly ground pepper, fresh sage, and/or a drizzle of extra virgin olive oil.

*Sweet, crisp apples, such as Fuji or Honey Crisp work particularly well in this recipe.

I left the skins on the apple and potatoes because it makes prep easier, and keeps all the good stuff found in the skins in the soup.

Turmeric can have a strong flavor. If it's new to you and your family, start with 1 teaspoon. If you love it, add more the next time.

Toppings really send this soup over the top, and turn it into a full meal. Top with Smokey Maple Roasted Chickpeas for a plant-based option, cooked chicken sausage for the meat-eaters, freshly ground pepper, fresh sage, and/or a drizzle of extra virgin olive oil. Freshly ground pepper brings out the nourishing benefits of turmeric, so feel free to add as much as you like when serving.

Nutrition Facts:

Serving: 1 (of 6) | Calories: 294kcal | Carbohydrates: 53g | Protein: 5g | Fat: 8g | Saturated Fat: 7g | Polyunsaturated Fat: 0.2g | Monounsaturated Fat: 0.4g | Sodium: 480mg | Potassium: 874mg | Fiber: 8g | Sugar: 16g | Vitamin A: 21492IU | Vitamin C: 12mg | Calcium: 70mg | Iron: 3mg

Slow Cooker Butternut Squash, Kale & Quinoa Stew

Cooking Time: 4 Hours

Servings: 6

Ingredients:

- 1 large yellow onion finely chopped
- 3 cups cubed butternut squash
- 3 garlic cloves minced or finely grated
- 1 teaspoon ground cumin
- ½ teaspoon smoked paprika
- 1-3 teaspoon kosher salt
- 1 (15-oz) can diced tomatoes
- 4 cups vegetable broth or chicken stock
- ½ cup dry quinoa
- To Add at the End
- 3 cups chopped kale
- 1 tablespoon white wine vinegar
- Fresh ground pepper, extra virgin olive oil, and parmesan (optional) for serving

Directions:

1. Combine the onion, butternut squash, garlic, cumin, paprika, salt, tomatoes, broth and quinoa in the base of a 6-quart slow cooker, stirring to combine.
2. Cover and cook for 4 hours on high or 6 hours on low, or until the onions and butternut squash are very tender and cooked through.
3. Uncover, add the kale, cover, and cook on high for the kale to wilt, about 15-20 minutes.
4. Uncover and add the vinegar, stirring to combine. Taste and additional salt or vinegar if you like.
5. Serve, drizzled with extra virgin olive and freshly ground pepper.

Notes

Serve with crusty bread for dunking.

If you eat dairy, sprinkle the soup with freshly grated parmesan cheese prior to serving.

Adapted for the slow cooker from Butternut Squash,

Kale and Quinoa Stew.

Nutrition Facts:

Serving: 1(of 6) | Calories: 117kcal | Carbohydrates: 23g | Protein: 5g | Fat: 2g | Saturated Fat: 0.2g | Polyunsaturated Fat: 1g | Monounsaturated Fat: 0.3g | Sodium: 411mg | Potassium: 487mg | Fiber: 5g | Sugar: 3g | Vitamin A: 10877IU | Vitamin C: 48mg | Calcium: 136mg | Iron: 2mg

Easy Slow Cooker Lentil Soup

Cooking Time: 4 Hours

Servings: 6

Ingredients:

- 1 medium yellow onion chopped
- 1 cup chopped celery
- 2 cups chopped carrot
- 2 cloves garlic minced or finely grated
- 1 ½ teaspoon kosher salt divided
- 1 ½ cups dry green lentils (or brown lentils) rinsed and picked over
- 1 (15-oz) can petite-diced tomatoes
- 6-8 cups vegetable stock or chicken stock
- 1 large bay leaf or 2 small bay leaves
- To Add at the End
- 4 cups baby spinach
- 1 teaspoon red wine vinegar
- Optional Serving Suggestions
- Extra virgin olive oil, freshly cracked pepper, freshly grated parmesan cheese (traditional or vegan), fresh parsley, red pepper flakes, crusty bread

Directions:

1. Slow Cooker **Directions:**
2. Add the onion, celery, carrot, garlic, 1 teaspoon salt, lentils, tomatoes, stock and bay leaf to a 6-quart slow cooker, stirring to combine. Do not add the spinach, it will be added at the end.
3. Cover and cook on high for 4-6 hours or on low for 6-8 hours, or until the veggies and lentils are soft.
4. Remove the lid, remove the bay leaf, add the vinegar, and stir to combine. Add an additional 1-2 cups of stock to thin the soup if necessary. Taste and add the remaining ½ teaspoon salt, plus additional vinegar if desired.
5. Using an immersion blender, blend for 5-10 seconds. Alternatively, carefully, remove ½ to 1 cup of cooked soup to a blender. Cover, blend on high, then add back to the soup, stirring to combine. Note: Blending for just a few seconds will add a creaminess to the soup, while leaving the texture of

most of the lentils and vegetables intact.

6. Add the spinach, and stir to combine. Serve with a generous drizzle of olive oil, and any other toppings you like.

7. Instant Pot **Directions:**

8. Set a 6-quart pressure cooker to saute mode for 8 minutes. Add 1 tablespoon olive oil, onion, a pinch of salt, and cook, stirring occasionally, until the onions are soft.

9. Cancel the saute function. Add the celery, carrot, garlic, 1 teaspoon salt, lentils, tomatoes, stock, and bay leaf, stirring to combine.

10. Secure the lid, select the manual setting, and set it to high pressure for 15 minutes.

11. When the pressure cooker timer is done, allow to naturally release for 15 minutes.

12. Follow remaining slow cooker steps 3-5.

13. Stovetop **Directions:**

14. Heat 1 tablespoon olive oil over medium high heat in a large Dutch oven. Add the onion and a pinch of salt, stirring to combine. Cook until the onions soften, about 8 minutes, stirring occasionally.

15. Add the celery, carrot, garlic, and 1 teaspoon salt, stirring to combine. Cook for an additional 2 minutes, stirring occasionally.

16. Add the lentils, tomatoes, bay leaf, and stock, stirring to combine. Cover, bring to a boil, then reduce to a simmer.

17. Cook, covered, until the lentils are soft, about 35-45 minutes, stirring occasionally.

18. Follow remaining slow cooker steps 3-5.

Notes

Dried brown or green lentils work interchangeably here. Do not use red lentils.

The heat of slow cookers can vary, as can the amount of liquid lentils absorb during the cooking process. If necessary add additional stock at the end, to achieve your desired consistency.

This soup will also thicken considerably as it cools, so if you prefer it thicker, allow to cool for 30 minutes prior to serving.

Sodium will very based on type of stock and tomatoes used. For a lower sodium option use low sodium stock and tomatoes.

Nutrition Facts:

Serving: 1 (of 6) | Calories: 241kcal | Carbohydrates: 45g | Protein: 15g | Fat: 1g | Saturated Fat: 1g | Polyunsaturated Fat: 1g | Monounsaturated Fat: 1g | Sodium: 776mg | Potassium: 983mg | Fiber: 18g | Sugar: 10g | Vitamin A: 9914IU | Vitamin C: 19mg | Calcium:

97mg | Iron: 5mg

Minestra Maritata (Italian Wedding Soup)

Servings: 6

Ingredients:

- 4 tablespoons extra-virgin olive oil, divided
- 1 1/3 cups chopped yellow onion
- 2/3 cup chopped carrot
- 2/3 cup chopped celery
- 2 tablespoons minced garlic
- 6 cups unsalted chicken broth
- 6 ounces orzo, preferably whole-wheat
- 1 ½ tablespoons chopped fresh oregano
- ½ teaspoon kosher salt
- 24 cooked chicken meatballs (12 ounces), such as Easy Chicken Meatballs
- 4 cups baby spinach
- ¼ cup grated Parmesan cheese

Directions:

1. Heat 1 tablespoon oil in a large pot or Dutch oven over medium-high heat. Add onion, carrot, celery and garlic; cook, stirring occasionally, until the onion is translucent, 4 to 5 minutes.
2. Add broth, cover and bring to a boil. Add orzo, oregano and salt; cover and cook, stirring occasionally, until the orzo is just tender, about 9 minutes.
3. Stir in meatballs and spinach; cook until the meatballs are heated through and the spinach is wilted, 2 to 4 minutes.
4. Serve sprinkled with cheese and drizzled with the remaining 3 tablespoons oil.

Nutrition Facts:

Calories 415 Total Carbohydrate 36g Dietary Fiber 4g Total Sugars 5g Protein 26g Total Fat 19g Saturated Fat 5g Cholesterol 101mg Vitamin A 5270iu Vitamin C 20mg Folate 23mcg Sodium 728mg Calcium 165mg Iron 3mg Magnesium 68mg Potassium 681mg

Hearty Chickpea & Spinach Stew

Servings: 4

Ingredients:

- 2 (15 ounce) cans low-sodium chickpeas, rinsed, divided
- 1 tablespoon olive oil
- 12 ounces 93%-lean ground turkey
- ½ teaspoon dried oregano
- ½ teaspoon fennel seeds, crushed

- ½ teaspoon crushed red pepper
- 1 medium onion, chopped (1 cup)
- 2 medium carrots, diced (3/4 cup)
- 4 cloves garlic, minced, or 1/2 teaspoon garlic powder
- 3 tablespoons tomato paste
- 1 (32 ounce) carton low-sodium chicken broth (4 cups)
- ¼ teaspoon ground pepper
- ⅛ teaspoon salt
- 3 cups IQF (individually quick-frozen) spinach (8 oz.)
- ¼ cup grated Parmesan cheese (Optional)

Directions:

1. Mash 1 can chickpeas with a potato masher or fork. Set aside.
2. Heat oil in a large pot over medium-high heat. Add turkey, oregano, fennel seeds and crushed red pepper. Cook, crumbling with a wooden spoon, until the turkey is no longer pink, 2 to 3 minutes. Add onion, carrots and garlic (or garlic powder). Cook, stirring often, until softened and fragrant, 3 to 4 minutes. Add tomato paste. Cook, stirring, for 30 seconds.
3. Add broth, the mashed and whole chickpeas, pepper and salt to the pot. Cover and bring to a simmer. Reduce heat to medium and cook, covered, at a brisk simmer until the vegetables are tender and the flavors have blended, about 10 minutes.
4. Add spinach and increase heat to medium-high, Cook, stirring, until the spinach is heated through, 1 to 2 minutes. Ladle the soup into bowls. Garnish each serving with 1 tablespoon Parmesan, if desired.

Tip

Individually quick-frozen (IQF) spinach makes this recipe a breeze. If you can't find it, use a frozen 10-ounce block of spinach. Cook according to the package directions, then add to the soup in Step 4.

Nutrition Facts:

Calories 401 Total Carbohydrate 41g Dietary Fiber 13g Total Sugars 10g Protein 32g Total Fat 13g Saturated Fat 3g Cholesterol 49mg Vitamin A 12057iu Vitamin C 11mg Folate 148mcg Sodium 643mg Calcium 180mg Iron 6mg Magnesium 114mg Potassium 982mg

Kale & Avocado Salad with Blueberries & Edamame

Servings: 4

Ingredients:

- 6 cups stemmed and coarsely chopped curly kale
- 1 avocado, diced
- 1 cup blueberries
- 1 cup halved yellow cherry tomatoes
- 1 cup cooked shelled edamame
- ¼ cup sliced almonds, toasted (see Tip)
- ½ cup crumbled goat cheese (2 ounces)
- ¼ cup olive oil
- 3 tablespoons lemon juice
- 1 tablespoon minced chives
- 1 ½ teaspoons honey
- 1 teaspoon Dijon mustard
- 1 teaspoon salt

Directions:

1. Place kale in a large bowl and, using your hands, massage to soften the leaves. Add avocado, blueberries, tomatoes, edamame, almonds, and goat cheese.
2. Combine oil, lemon juice, chives, honey, mustard, and salt in a small bowl or in a jar with a tight-fitting lid. Whisk or shake well.
3. Drizzle the vinaigrette over the salad and toss to combine.

Tips

To make ahead: Wash, stem, and chop kale, cook edamame, toast almonds, and make vinaigrette (Step 2) up to 1 day ahead and refrigerate.

Tip: To toast sliced (or chopped) nuts, place in a small dry skillet and cook over medium-low heat, stirring constantly, until fragrant, 2 to 4 minutes.

Nutrition Facts:

Calories 368 Total Carbohydrate 21g Dietary Fiber 8g Total Sugars 9g Protein 10g Total Fat 29g Saturated Fat 5g Cholesterol 10mg Sodium 674mg Potassium 692mg

One-Pot Lentil & Vegetable Soup with Parmesan

Servings: 6

Ingredients:

- 2 tablespoons extra-virgin olive oil
- 3 cups fresh or frozen chopped onion, carrot and celery mix
- 4 cloves garlic, chopped
- 4 cups low-sodium vegetable or chicken broth

- 1 ½ cups green or brown lentils
- 1 (15-ounce) can unsalted diced tomatoes, undrained
- 2 teaspoons finely chopped fresh thyme
- ½ teaspoon salt
- ½ teaspoon ground pepper
- ½ teaspoon crushed red pepper
- ½ cup grated Parmesan cheese
- Parmesan rind (optional)
- 3 cups packed roughly chopped lacinato kale
- 1 ½ tablespoons red-wine vinegar
- Chopped fresh flat-leaf parsley for garnish

Directions:

1. Heat oil in a Dutch oven or large pot over medium heat. Add onion, carrot and celery mix; cook, stirring occasionally, until softened, 6 to 10 minutes. Add garlic; cook, stirring often, until fragrant, about 30 seconds.
2. Stir in broth, lentils, tomatoes, thyme, salt, pepper, crushed red pepper and Parmesan rind, if using. Bring to a boil over medium-high heat. Reduce heat to medium-low; cover and cook, stirring occasionally, until the lentils are almost tender, 15 to 25 minutes, adding water as needed to thin to desired consistency.
3. Stir in kale. Cook, covered, until the kale is tender, 5 to 10 minutes. Remove and discard the Parmesan rind, if using. Stir in vinegar. Divide the soup among 6 bowls; sprinkle with Parmesan. Garnish with parsley, if desired.
4. To make ahead
5. Refrigerate for up to 5 days or freeze for up to 2 months.

Nutrition Facts:

Calories 306 Total Carbohydrate 45g Dietary Fiber 9g Total Sugars 6g Protein 17g Total Fat 7g Saturated Fat 2g Cholesterol 5mg Vitamin A 6301iu Sodium 446mg Potassium 489mg

Egg Drop Soup with Instant Noodles, Spinach & Scallions

Servings: 1

Ingredients:

- 2 cups water
- ½ (3 ounce) package rice-noodle soup mix, such as Thai Kitchen Garlic & Vegetable
- 1 large egg
- 1 cup baby spinach
- 1 scallion, sliced

Directions:

1. Bring water to a boil in a small saucepan. Stir in half of the seasoning packet (discard the remainder or reserve for another use). Add noodles and cook until tender, about 3 minutes. Reduce heat to maintain a simmer.
2. Whisk egg in a small bowl. Slowly pour the egg into the simmering soup, stirring constantly. Fold in spinach until just wilted, about 30 seconds. Transfer to a bowl and sprinkle with scallion.

Nutrition Facts:

Calories 258 Total Carbohydrate 37g Dietary Fiber 2g Total Sugars 3g Added Sugars 2g Protein 11g Total Fat 7g Saturated Fat 2g Cholesterol 186mg Vitamin A 4086iu Vitamin C 19mg Folate 33mcg Sodium 131mg Calcium 106mg Iron 3mg Magnesium 54mg Potassium 115mg

Slow-Cooker Mediterranean Diet Stew

Servings: 6

Ingredients:

- 2 (14 ounce) cans no-salt-added fire-roasted diced tomatoes
- 3 cups low-sodium vegetable broth
- 1 cup coarsely chopped onion
- ¾ cup chopped carrot
- 4 cloves garlic, minced
- 1 teaspoon dried oregano
- ¾ teaspoon salt
- ½ teaspoon crushed red pepper
- ¼ teaspoon ground pepper
- 1 (15 ounce) can no-salt-added chickpeas, rinsed, divided
- 1 bunch lacinato kale, stemmed and chopped (about 8 cups)
- 1 tablespoon lemon juice
- 3 tablespoons extra-virgin olive oil
- Fresh basil leaves, torn if large
- 6 lemon wedges (Optional)

Directions:

1. Combine tomatoes, broth, onion, carrot, garlic, oregano, salt, crushed red pepper and pepper in a 4-quart slow cooker. Cover and cook on Low for 6 hours.
2. Measure 1/4 cup of the cooking liquid from the slow cooker into a small bowl. Add 2 tablespoons chickpeas; mash with a fork until smooth.
3. Add the mashed chickpeas, kale, lemon juice and remaining whole chickpeas to the mixture in the slow cooker. Stir to combine. Cover and cook on

Low until the kale is tender, about 30 minutes.

4. Ladle the stew evenly into 6 bowls; drizzle with oil. Garnish with basil. Serve with lemon wedges, if desired.

Nutrition Facts:

Calories 191 Total Carbohydrate 23g   Dietary Fiber 6g Total Sugars 7g   Protein 6g   Total Fat 8g   Saturated Fat 1g   Vitamin A 5380iu   Vitamin C 33mg   Folate 39mcg   Sodium 416mg   Calcium 128mg   Iron 2mg   Magnesium 34mg   Potassium 310mg

Chicken & Kale Soup

Servings: 6

Ingredients:

- 1 tablespoon extra-virgin olive oil
- 1 ½ cups chopped yellow onion
- 1 tablespoon minced garlic
- 1 (15 ounce) can no-salt-added great northern beans, rinsed
- 12 ounces boneless, skinless chicken breast or chicken tenders
- 2 medium Yukon Gold potatoes, peeled and diced (1/2-inch)
- 6 cups unsalted chicken broth
- 3 thyme sprigs
- 1 teaspoon kosher salt
- ½ teaspoon ground pepper
- 3 cups chopped kale or 1 (10 ounce) package frozen chopped kale
- 2 tablespoons lemon juice

Directions:

1. Heat oil in a large, heavy pot over medium heat. Add onion; cook, stirring occasionally, until softened, about 5 minutes. Add garlic; cook, stirring constantly, until fragrant, about 1 minute. Add beans, chicken, potatoes, broth, thyme, salt and pepper. Bring to a boil over medium-high heat; reduce heat to maintain a simmer. Simmer, covered, until the potatoes are tender and an instant-read thermometer inserted in the thickest portion of the chicken registers 165°F, about 18 minutes.

2. Transfer the chicken to a plate and, using 2 forks, shred it into bite-size pieces. Stir kale into the soup; cook over medium heat, stirring often, until the kale is wilted and tender, about 2 minutes. Remove from heat; stir in the shredded chicken and lemon juice. Remove the thyme sprigs before serving. Serve hot.

Nutrition Facts:

Calories 271 Total Carbohydrate 30g   Dietary Fiber 7g

Total Sugars 5g   Protein 26g   Total Fat 5g   Saturated Fat 1g   Cholesterol 48mg   Vitamin A 837iu   Vitamin C 22mg   Folate 50mcg   Sodium 531mg   Calcium 89mg   Iron 2mg   Magnesium 65mg   Potassium 879mg

Vegetable Soup

Cooking Time: 20 Mins.

Servings: 8

Ingredients:

- 2 tbsp of extra virgin olive oil
- 3 cloves garlic, chopped
- 1 large onion chooped
- 3 large carrots chopped
- 2 ribs celery chopped
- 1 large zucchini chopped
- 1 28 ounce diced tomato
- 4 cups vegetable stock
- 1 tbsp paprika
- 1/2 tbsp smoked paprika
- 1 tsp dried oregano
- 1 tsp sea salt
- 1 tsp black pepper
- 2 tsp of coconut palm sugar
- 2 cups fresh corn kernels (frozen will also work)
- 2 cups kale, chopped
- Toppings
- fresh chopped cilantro
- squeeze of fresh lime juice

Directions:

1. In a large soup pot, over medium heat, saute garlic, onion, carrot, and celery until tender (about 7 minutes) stirring frequently. Add a generous pinch of salt and pepper.
2. Add chopped zucchini, diced tomato, vegetable stock, dried spices, and coconut palm sugar. Stir to combine. Allow to come to a boil, reduce heat and simmer for 15 minutes
3. Add corn and kale. Cook for an additional 5 minutes
4. Serve in a beautiful bowl topped with a squeeze of lime juice and fresh chopped cilantro

Notes

Substitutions

You can substitute just about any vegetables you like some additons that I've tried that work very well: green beans, yellow squash, spinach, fennel, parsnips, bell peppers, and sweet potato.

Nutrition Facts:

Calories: 130kcal | Carbohydrates: 22g | Protein: 3g | Fat: 4g | Sodium: 662mg | Potassium: 586mg | Fiber: 3g |

Sugar: 10g | Vitamin A: 6675IU | Vitamin C: 39.2mg | Calcium: 82mg | Iron: 2mg

Thai Carrot Soup

Cooking Time: 30 Mins.

Servings: 6

Ingredients:

- 1 tablespoon coconut oil
- 1 large white onion, chopped
- 5 cups carrots, chopped
- 5 cloves garlic, chopped
- 1 tablespoon fresh ginger, finely diced
- 1/2 tsp sea salt
- 1 tablespoon coconut palm sugar or brown sugar
- 1 tablespoon Thai red curry paste I like the brand Thai Kitchen
- 13.5 ounces light coconut milk (1 can)
- 3 cups vegetable stock
- Sriracha sauce optional

Directions:

1. In a large soup pot over medium heat melt coconut oil. Add onion, carrots, garlic, and ginger and saute for 5-6 minutes or until the vegetables begin to soften.
2. Add salt and Thai red curry paste to the pot and stir well to coat vegetables. Slowly add in coconut milk, and coconut palm sugar, stir well to dissolve curry paste.
3. Add vegetable stock, partially cover the pot, reduce heat to medium-low and cook for 15-20 minutes or until the vegetables are completely soft.
4. Taste for seasoning adding more salt if needed, Puree soup using a stick blender or by transferring to a high-speed blender. Blend until completely smooth.
5. Serve soup with a small drizzle of Sriracha sauce and an extra swirl of coconut milk.

Notes

Recipe Notes and Tips:

Stock - You can use vegetable or chicken stock or I often use bone broth.

Thai Red Curry Paste keeps well in the refrigerator for 2-3 weeks. You can also make this Thai Vegetable Curry recipe with it!

Nutrition Facts:

Serving: 1bowl | Calories: 147kcal | Carbohydrates: 19g | Protein: 1g | Fat: 7g | Saturated Fat: 6g | Sodium: 796mg | Potassium: 388mg | Fiber: 4g | Sugar: 9g | Vitamin A: 18464IU | Vitamin C: 9mg | Calcium: 49mg | Iron: 1mg

Super Green Detoxifying Broccoli Soup

Cooking Time: 20 Mins.

Servings: 6

Ingredients:

- 1 tbsp olive oil
- 2 stalks celery, diced about 1 cup
- 1 medium onion, diced about 1 cup
- 4 cloves garlic sliced
- 1 large head broccoli stems and tops separated. About 6 cups of florets and 2-3 cups of stems
- 1 tsp turmeric
- 1/4 tsp sea salt
- 1/4 tsp black pepper
- 6 cups vegetable stock
- 4-6 cups leafy greens spinach, kale, or swiss chard
- 3 tbsp nutritional yeast
- 1 tbsp hemp seeds (optional, for garnish)

Directions:

1. In a large stockpot over medium heat saute onion, celery, garlic, and broccoli stems for 5 minutes in olive oil. Add turmeric, salt, and pepper. Saute additional 1 minute.
2. Add stock and broccoli florets, bring to a simmer and cook for 15 minutes or until broccoli is tender.
3. Add leafy greens and allow to wilt (about 1 minute). (optional: reserve a bit of the wilted greens and broccoli florets for garnish)
4. Transfer soup to a blender (or use an immersion blender directly in the pot) add nutritional yeast and puree until smooth and creamy.
5. Serve topped with wilted greens and florets and a sprinkle of hemp seeds.

Notes

STORAGE + REHEATING + FREEZING INSTRUCTIONS:

STORAGE - Store in an airtight container in the refrigerator for up to 5 days (I often fill mason jars with this magic soup for easy to grab goodness)

REHEATING - Reheat in a small saucepan over medium heat until warmed throughout. If you must use a microwave, go for it but stovetop is better to help preserve all of the nutrients

FREEZING - Freeze in an airtight container, or mason jar (if using a mason jar fill only 3/4 of the way full, freeze without the top, and then add the top once frozen. Will keep in the fridge for up to 3 months.

DEFROST - Defrost in the fridge overnight, reheat on stovetop. Some natural separation will occur, just stir well when reheating.

Nutrition Facts:

Serving: 1serving (6 total Servings: in recipe) | Calories: 125kcal | Carbohydrates: 16g | Protein: 7g | Fat: 5g | Saturated Fat: 1g | Polyunsaturated Fat: 2g | Monounsaturated Fat: 2g | Sodium: 1106mg | Potassium: 630mg | Fiber: 6g | Sugar: 5g | Vitamin A: 5668IU | Vitamin C: 135mg | Calcium: 179mg | Iron: 2mg

Greek Lentil Jar Salad

Cooking Time: 35 Mins.

Servings: 4

Ingredients:

- 1 cup dried lentils or 1 cup prepared cooked lentils
- 1 cup radishes
- 1 cup roasted red peppers
- 2 cups arugula
- 1/4 cup scallions
- 1/4 cup kalamata olives
- 1/2 cup grape tomatoes
- 1/2 cup feta cheese
- Dijon Vinaigrette
- 4 tbsp extra virgin olive oil
- 2 tbsp fresh lemon juice
- 1 tsp dijon mustard
- 1 clove garlic, crushed
- 1/4 tsp sea salt
- 1/4 tsp black pepper
- 1/8 tsp dried oregano

Directions:

1. Lentils
2. Rinse the lentils in a fine mesh sieve, make sure to inspect for any bad lentils or little stones.
3. Add lentils to a large pot and fill with water. Add any aromatics you like (1 bay leaf will do the trick!) Bring the pot to a boil, reduce to a simmer and cook for 20-30 minutes. Test the lentils at 20 minutes by tasting them. When they are tender they are done.
4. Drain the lentils, remove the bay leaves, and set aside to cool
5. Dijon Vinaigrette
6. Combine all dressing ingredients and whisk well until emulsified and "creamy". Set aside.
7. Assemble the salad (divide ingredients between 4 jars)
8. Assemble the jar salad with dressing on the bottom, followed by lentils, radishes, red peppers, olives, arugula, tomato, and feta cheese.
9. When ready to eat simply shake or stir well to combine dressing with ingredients.

Nutrition Facts:

Calories: 378kcal | Carbohydrates: 35g | Protein: 16g | Fat: 20g | Saturated Fat: 5g | Cholesterol: 17mg | Sodium: 999mg | Potassium: 687mg | Fiber: 16g | Sugar: 3g | Vitamin A: 768IU | Vitamin C: 31mg | Calcium: 166mg | Iron: 4mg

Escarole Citrus Salad with Meyer Lemon Vinaigrette

Servings: 4

Ingredients:

- 1 head escarole washed and torn into bite size pieces
- 1 medium grapefruit
- 1 medium blood orange
- 1 small tangerine
- 1/2 cup fennel, thinly sliced
- 1/4 cup radish, thinly sliced
- 1 small avocado, sliced
- 1 tbsp fresh chives
- Meyer Lemon Vinaigrette
- 1/4 cup California Olive Ranch extra virgin olive oil
- 1/4 cup freshly squeezed meyer lemon juice
- 1/4 tsp raw honey
- generous pinch sea salt

Directions:

1. Dressing
2. Add all ingredients to OXO Salad Dressing Shaker and shake vigorously.
3. Salad
4. Segment Citrus: Begin by slicing a little off of the top and bottom of the citrus fruit. Trim away the skin and the pith, by starting at the top of the fruit and slicing downward following the curve of the fruit. Once all of the skin and pith is removed you can either slice into rounds or segment. To segment: use a paring knife, slip the knife between one of the segments and the connective membrane, cut until you reach the middle of the fruit, scoop the segment out and continue until all segments are released from the connective membrane.
5. Arrange escarole on a platter. Top with citrus, fennel, radish, and avocado slices. Drizzle with Meyer Lemon Vinaigrette and scatter the top with chopped chives.

Notes

You can use any citrus that you love in this recipe. Grapefruit, blood orange, and tangerine are my favorites, but a simple orange would also be lovely.

Nutrition Facts:

Calories: 266kcal | Carbohydrates: 20g | Protein: 3g | Fat: 21g | Saturated Fat: 3g | Sodium: 37mg | Potassium: 792mg | Fiber: 8g | Sugar: 8g | Vitamin A: 3425IU | Vitamin C: 47.9mg | Calcium: 91mg | Iron: 1.4mg

Farmers Market Lentil Salad

Cooking Time: 35 Mins.

Servings: 4

Ingredients:

- Salad
- 1 cup dry black beluga lentils
- 4 cups water
- 2 sprigs fresh oregano
- 1 tsp sea salt
- 1 cup diced radish
- 1 cup chopped radish tops
- 1 cup diced sugar snap peas
- 1 cup diced cherry tomatoes
- 1 cup sliced fresh cherries
- 1/2 avocado sliced
- Spicy Lime Dressing
- 2 tbsp fresh lime juice
- 2 tbsp olive oil
- 1/2 tsp salt
- 1 1/2 tsp honey
- 1/4 tsp crushed red pepper

Directions:

1. To cook the lentils: pick through the lentils and remove any debris or small stones (don't skip this step it could cost you a broken tooth). Rinse lentils in a fine mesh sieve under running water. Add lentils to a medium saucepan, cover with water and 1 sprig of fresh oregano. Bring to a boil over medium-high heat.
2. Reduce heat to medium-low and allow lentils to simmer for 25-35 minutes or until tender. Strain lentils and set aside to cool.
3. In the meantime, combine radishes, radish tops, sugar snap peas, cherry tomatoes, and fresh cherries in a large bowl.
4. To prepare the dressing whisk together lime juice, honey, olive oil, and crushed red pepper. Set aside.
5. Once the lentils have cooled, add them to the bowl with veggies, pour dressing over salad and stir well to combine. Add sliced avocado on top, sprinkle avocado with crushed red pepper and sprinkle fresh (or dried) oregano on top of entire salad. Taste for seasoning, add more salt if needed

Nutrition Facts:

Calories: 325kcal | Carbohydrates: 41g | Protein: 16g |

Fat: 11g | Saturated Fat: 1g | Sodium: 908mg | Potassium: 396mg | Fiber: 13g | Sugar: 9g | Vitamin A: 545IU | Vitamin C: 84.6mg | Calcium: 232mg | Iron: 5.1mg

Mediterranean Farro Salad with Roasted Eggplant

Cooking Time: 40 Mins.

Servings: 6

Ingredients:

- 1 cup farro
- 1 medium eggplant diced into 1" pieces
- 1 medium red bell pepper chopped
- 1 large red onion chopped
- 8 cloves garlic cut in half
- 1/4 cup extra virgin olive oil
- 1/2 tsp sea salt
- 1/2 tsp black pepper
- 2 cups cherry tomatoes quartered
- 1/2 cup fresh herbs (parsley, dill, and a few sprigs of fresh thyme)
- 1/2 cup kalamata olives sliced
- 2 tbsp capers
- Garlic Vinaigrette
- 3 tbsp extra virgin olive oil
- 1 tbsp red wine vinegar
- 1 tbsp fresh lemon juice
- 1/2 tsp dijon mustard
- 1 clove garlic, crushed
- 1/4 tsp salt
- 1/4 tsp black pepper

Directions:

1. To cook farro: Bring 4 cups of water to a boil in a medium to large pot. Add salt when water just begins to boil. Add farro and cook for 30-40 minutes until tender. Drain and set aside. *see note for soaked farro cooking time*
2. While farro is cooking roast vegetables: Toss eggplant, red pepper, red onion, and garlic with olive oil, salt and pepper. Spread out on a sheet pan in a single layer. Roast in a 350° oven for 40 minutes, tossing several times during roasting.
3. Prepare vinaigrette by whisking together all **Ingredients:**
4. Toss together farro, roasted vegetables, tomato, fresh herbs, capers, olives, and vinaigrette.
5. Will keep for 6 days in a sealed container in the refrigerator.

Notes

Farro:

I prefer to soak farro prior to cooking, this step is

optional but I find it increases the digestibility and produces a superior product. To soak: Cover farro with water and allow to soak for 30-50 minutes. Drain and set aside. Soaked farro will cook quicker typically 20-25 minutes.

Substitutions:

Gluten Free: Try using quinoa or brown rice instead of farro

Paleo: Try using cauliflower rice instead of farro

Nutrition Facts:

Calories: 399kcal | Carbohydrates: 37g | Protein: 9g | Fat: 25g | Saturated Fat: 2g | Sodium: 563mg | Potassium: 404mg | Fiber: 8g | Sugar: 3g | Vitamin A: 910IU | Vitamin C: 40.4mg | Calcium: 81mg | Iron: 3.3mg

Super Seed Salad Topper

Cooking Time: 15 Mins.

Servings: 22

Ingredients:

- 1/2 cup pumpkin seeds
- 1/2 cup sunflower seeds
- 1/2 cup sesame seeds, flaxseed, chia seed, hemp seed 1 or a combination of all
- 1 tbsp coconut oil or avocado oil
- 2 tsp coconut palm sugar
- 1/4 tsp sea salt
- pinch cayenne pepper (optional)

Directions:

1. Line a large baking sheet with parchment paper. Combine all seeds with coconut oil, salt, coconut palm sugar, and a pinch of cayenne pepper.
2. Roast in a 300° oven for 15 minutes
3. Store in a sealed container in the refrigerator for up to 1 month.

Notes

Seeds - you can use any variety of seeds that you like

Spices - I love a little hint of spicy, sweet, and salty - but you can eliminate any one of those flavors

Nutrition Facts:

Serving: 1tablespoon | Calories: 52kcal | Carbohydrates: 2g | Protein: 2g | Fat: 5g | Saturated Fat: 1g | Sodium: 28mg | Potassium: 47mg | Fiber: 1g | Sugar: 1g | Vitamin C: 1mg | Calcium: 36mg | Iron: 1mg

Red Cabbage Vegetable Quinoa Stew

Cooking Time: 40 Mins.

Servings: 10

Ingredients:

- 1 tbsp olive oil
- 1 large onion, chopped
- 2 stalks celery, chopped
- 2 large carrots, chopped
- 3 cloves garlic, chopped
- 2 tsp freshly grated turmeric (or 2 tsp turmeric powder)
- 1 tsp sea salt
- 1/4 tsp ground black pepper
- 1/2 tsp dried oregano
- 2 bay leaves
- 1 cup sweet potato, diced (about 1 medium sweet potato)
- 1/2 small red cabbage, chopped
- 4 cups vegetable stock
- 28 oz whole peeled tomato (canned)
- 2 cups water
- 3/4 cup quinoa
- 1 can chickpeas (15 ounce can)
- 3 cups baby kale
- fresh lemon juice for serving

Directions:

1. In a large soup pot over medium heat saute onion, celery, garlic, and carrot in olive oil for 5 minutes.
2. Add fresh turmeric (or dried), sea salt, black pepper, oregano, bay leaves, sweet potato, and red cabbage. Saute for 2 minutes.
3. Add vegetable stock, tomato (I crush each whole tomato in my fist prior to adding it to the pot, alternatively you can use diced tomato), and water, stir well. Add quinoa, bring to a boil, reduce heat and simmer for 25 minutes.
4. Add chickpeas and kale, simmer for 5 more minutes.
5. Finish with 2 tbsp of fresh lemon juice. Serve each bowl with additional lemon juice.

Nutrition Facts:

Serving: 1large bowl | Calories: 124kcal | Carbohydrates: 22g | Protein: 4g | Fat: 2g | Sodium: 765mg | Potassium: 536mg | Fiber: 3g | Sugar: 5g | Vitamin A: 6945IU | Vitamin C: 50.6mg | Calcium: 92mg | Iron: 2.2mg

Spring Green Salad

Servings: 4

Ingredients:

- ¼ cup plain whole-milk Greek yogurt
- ¼ cup fresh lemon juice (from 2 lemons)
- 1 teaspoon kosher salt
- ½ teaspoon freshly ground black pepper
- 1 anchovy fillet
- 2 ripe avocados, peeled and pitted, divided
- ½ cup chopped fresh chives, divided
- 4 tablespoons chopped fresh mint, divided
- 2 romaine hearts, chopped
- ½ English cucumber, chopped
- 1 cup sugar snap peas, halved
- ½ cup frozen shelled edamame, thawed
- 1/3 cup shelled roasted salted pistachios, chopped

Directions:

1. Process yogurt, lemon juice, 1 tablespoon water, salt, pepper, anchovy, 1 avocado, ¼ cup chives, and 2 tablespoons mint in a blender until smooth. Add more water, 1 tablespoon at a time, until just pourable.
2. Chop the remaining avocado and place it in a large bowl. Add romaine, cucumber, snap peas, and edamame. Toss with half the dressing. Top with pistachios and remaining ¼ cup chives and 2 tablespoons mint. Serve the remaining dressing on the side.

Farro and Squash Salad

Servings: 8

Ingredients:

- 1 1/2 cups farro
- 2 tbsp balsamic vinegar
- 1 1/2 tsp. salt
- 6 tbsp olive oil
- 4 medium yellow squash and/or zucchini, trimmed and halved lengthwise
- 1/2 cup roughly chopped almonds (preferably Marcona), plus more for topping
- 1/4 cups grated Parmesan cheese
- 1/4 cup basil leaves

Directions:

1. Cook farro in salted water according to package directions. Drain and transfer to a large bowl. Let cool for 10 minutes, stirring occasionally.
2. Whisk vinegar, salt, and 5 tablespoons oil in a large bowl until combined. Add half of dressing to farro; toss to coat.
3. Preheat grill to medium-high (400°F to 450°F).

Brush squash with remaining 1 tablespoon oil. Place squash, cut side down, on grates; grill, covered, until tender and charred, 3 to 4 minutes per side. Transfer to a cutting board and let cool for 5 minutes.

4. Cut squash diagonally into 1-inch pieces. Place in bowl with remaining dressing; toss to coat. Add almonds and cheese to cooled farro; toss to coat. Spoon onto a platter in an even layer. Top with squash, then with basil and more almonds and cheese.

Nutrition Facts:

Calories 249 Total Fat 16g Saturated Fat 2g Cholesterol 3mg Sodium 534mg Total Carbohydrate 23g Dietary Fiber 5g Total Sugars 7g Protein 7g Vitamin C 10mg Calcium 100mg Iron 2mg Potassium 470mg

Coconut Ranch Kale Salad

Servings: 2 - 4

Ingredients:

- FOR COCONUT RANCH
- 1/4 c. coconut milk
- 1/4 c. vegan mayonaise
- 1 tbsp. freshly chopped parsley
- 1 tbsp. freshly chopped chives
- 2 tsp. freshly chopped dill
- 1/2 tsp. garlic powder
- 1/4 tsp. onion powder
- Pinch cayenne pepper
- Kosher salt
- Freshly ground black pepper
- FOR SALAD:
- 1 large sweet potato, cut in 1/4" thick half moons
- 1 tbsp. plus 2 tsp extra-virgin olive oil, divided
- 1 1/2 tsp. chili powder, divided
- Kosher salt
- Freshly ground black pepper
- 1 (15-oz.) can chickpeas, drained and rinsed
- 1 large bunch curly kale, washed and dried, stems removed
- Avocado, thinly sliced
- Shaved vegan parmesan

Directions:

1. In a small bowl, whisk together coconut milk and mayonnaise. Add herbs, garlic powder, onion powder, and a pinch of cayenne. Stir to combine, then season with salt and pepper. Refrigerate until ready to use.

2. Preheat oven to 400°. Place sweet potatoes on a large baking sheet and drizzle with 1 tablespoon oil and season with 1 teaspoon chili powder, salt, and pepper. Toss to coat, then spread potato slices out in an even layer.

3. Bake until tender and bottoms start to crisp, 35 to 40 minutes.

4. Pat chickpeas dry with a paper towel and place on a small baking sheet. Bake until dried out and crisp, 30 minutes.

5. While chickpeas are still warm, place in a medium bowl. Add remaining 2 teaspoons oil and ½ teaspoon chili powder. Toss to combine and season with salt and pepper.

6. Place dried kale on a cutting board and roughly chop into bite sized pieces. Place in a large bowl. Add a large pinch of salt and massage kale with your fingers, rubbing the salt in for about 1 minutes.

7. Top kale with sweet potatoes, chickpeas, avocado, and parmesan. Drizzle with coconut ranch to serve.

Niçoise Salad

Servings: 4

Ingredients:

- FOR SALAD
- Kosher salt
- 4 large eggs
- 1/2 lb. green beans, trimmed
- 1/2 lb. small potatoes
- 16 oz. tuna packed in olive oil
- 3 Persian cucumbers, sliced into 1/2" rounds
- 1/2 c. black olives, such as Kalamata
- 8 anchovy fillets packed in oil, drained (optional)
- 2 tbsp. capers, drained
- Basil leaves, for garnish
- FOR DRESSING
- 1/3 c. extra-virgin olive oil
- 3 tbsp. sherry vinegar
- 2 tbsp. Oil from jarred or canned tuna
- 1 clove garlic, grated or minced
- 1 tbsp. Dijon mustard
- 1 tsp. honey
- Freshly ground black pepper

Directions:

1. Prepare an ice bath in a medium bowl and bring a medium pot of water to a boil over high heat. Reduce heat to a low boil and use a spoon to carefully lower the eggs into the water. Cook for 8 minutes, then use a slotted spoon to transfer the eggs to an ice bath to cool. Turn off heat, and reserve the water.
2. Meanwhile, make dressing: Whisk all dressing ingredients together in a medium bowl and season to taste with salt and pepper.
3. Prepare another ice bath in a medium bowl. Return pot of water to high heat, add a large pinch of salt, and bring back to a boil. Add green beans and cook until bright green and just tender, about 3 to 5 minutes. Transfer to ice bath to cool, then transfer to a clean kitchen towel or paper towels. Reserve ice bath and pat green beans dry.
4. Add potatoes to boiling water and cook until tender, about 15 minutes. Drain.
5. Meanwhile, peel and halve hard-boiled eggs, and halve boiled potatoes. Drain remaining oil from tuna (saving if desired) and break tuna into large flakes.
6. To serve: Divide eggs, green beans, potatoes, tuna, cucumbers, and olives between 4 large plates. Lay an anchovy fillet on each egg half, if using. Top with capers, drizzle with dressing, and season with salt and pepper. Serve garnished with basil leaves and additional dressing on the side.

Burrata Salad

Servings: 4

Ingredients:

- 3 lb. heirloom or beefsteak tomatoes (about 4 large), sliced into 1/2" rounds
- 1 shallot, finely chopped
- Flaky sea salt
- Freshly ground black pepper
- 2 tbsp. extra-virgin olive oil
- 2 tbsp. red wine vinegar
- 1/3 c. panko bread crumbs
- 2 (4-oz.) balls burrata, drained and room temperature
- 1 tbsp. chopped fresh basil
- 1 tbsp. sliced fresh chives
- Crusty bread, for serving

Directions:

1. On a rimmed baking sheet, toss tomatoes and shallot; season with 1 teaspoon salt and 1 teaspoon pepper. Drizzle oil and vinegar over. Let sit until

tomatoes have released their liquid and shallots are softened, about 30 minutes.

2. In a small skillet over low heat, toast panko, stirring occasionally, until golden brown, about 2 minutes. Transfer to a small bowl.

3. Layer tomatoes on a large platter. Spoon shallot and juices over top. Sprinkle with panko. Arrange burrata in center of tomatoes and crack open with your hands. Sprinkle with basil, chives, salt, and pepper. Serve with bread alongside.

Greek Salmon Salad

Servings: 4

Ingredients:

- FOR THE SALMON
- 1 lb. salmon
- Kosher salt
- Freshly ground black pepper
- Pinch crushed red pepper flakes
- Juice of 1/2 lemon
- 1 tbsp. extra-virgin olive oil
- 1 clove garlic
- 1 tbsp. freshly chopped dill
- FOR THE DRESSING
- 1/2 c. Greek yogurt, preferably whole fat
- 2 tbsp. tahini
- Juice of 1/2 lemon
- 2 tbsp. warm water
- Kosher salt
- Freshly ground black pepper
- FOR THE SALAD
- 5 oz. baby spinach
- 1 head romaine, chopped
- 1 Persian cucumber, sliced
- 1 red bell pepper, sliced
- 1 c. cherry tomatoes, halved
- 1/2 c. kalamata olives, pitted and halved
- 1 avocado, sliced
- 1/2 c. pickled red onions
- 1/2 c. crumbled feta
- Freshly chopped dill
- Lemon wedges

Directions:

1. Preheat oven to 350° and line a small baking sheet with foil. Place salmon on foil and season with salt, pepper, and a pinch red pepper flakes.

2. In a small bowl, combine lemon juice, oil, garlic, and dill. Pour over salmon.

3. Bake until salmon is fork tender and internal temperature reaches 145°, about 35 minutes.

4. Meanwhile, make dressing: In a medium bowl, combine yogurt and tahini, then add lemon juice. Add warm water and stir to loosen. Add more water or lemon juice to thin dressing to desired consistency. Season with salt and pepper.

5. Assemble salad: Toss spinach, romaine, cucumber, bell pepper, tomatoes, and olives together. Break salmon into large pieces with a fork and top salad with it. Top with avocado, pickled onions, and feta. Garnish with dill and serve with dressing and lemon wedges.

Printed in Great Britain
by Amazon